10/06

5/16/08
BOOK WAS BENT
IN MIDDLE.

Teen Eating Disorders

Look for these and other books in the Lucent
Teen Issues series:

Teen Alcoholism
Teen Depression
Teen Drug Abuse
Teen Pregnancy
Teen Prostitution
Teen Sexuality
Teen Smoking
Teen Suicide
Teen Violence

Teen Eating Disorders

by Elizabeth Weiss Vollstadt

TEEN ISSUES

LUCENT *Overview Series*

LUCENT *Overview Series*

Library of Congress Cataloging-in-Publication Data

Vollstadt, Elizabeth Weiss, 1942–
  Teen eating disorders / Elizabeth Weiss Vollstadt.
    p.   cm. — (Lucent overview series. Teen issues)
  Includes bibliographical references and index.
  Summary: Discusses such topics as the causes of eating disorders,
dangers they represent, possible prevention techniques, and treat-
ment options.
  ISBN 1-56006-516-8 (lib. : alk. paper)
  1. Eating disorders in adolescence—Juvenile literature.   2. Teen-
agers—Health and hygiene—Juvenile literature.   [1. Eating disorders.]
I. Title.   II. Series.
RJ506.E18W45   1999
616.85'26'00835—dc21   99-10031
                                                              CIP

Copyright © 1999 by Lucent Books, Inc.
P.O. Box 289011, San Diego, CA 92198-9011
Printed in the U.S.A.

To Peter, for the gift of time.

Acknowledgments

My thanks to Kathy's mother, Paulette, for sharing her daughter's story with me. My thanks, too, to Dr. Joanne Witkowski, for reviewing this book for me. Dr. Witkowski is chief of the Department of Psychiatry at Kaiser Permanente Medical Center in Riverside, California, and co-chair of the Eating Disorder Task Force of the Southern California Permanente Medical Group.

Contents

Introduction

ALL TEENS ARE concerned about how they look. They want to be attractive and to fit in with others. But meeting society's standards for looking good isn't always easy, especially for girls. Girls are judged by their appearance more than boys are, and the standards are high. As always, physical attractiveness in females is based on pretty features, a good complexion, nice hair, and a well-proportioned body. Today, however, "well-proportioned" is popularly interpreted to mean "thin." As a result, many teenage girls are unhappy with their bodies. This is especially true of those who, because of pressures or problems in their own lives, become fixated on weight as a way of achieving success or happiness.

As Dan Rather reported in a *48 Hours* documentary,

> Women are far more likely than men to be unhappy with the way they look, and their weight is the biggest reason why. The worrying starts early. Nearly half of all 13-year-old girls say they don't like their looks. By 18, it's up to 80 percent. One study even found that young girls are more afraid of being fat than of nuclear war or getting cancer.[1]

The result of this preoccupation with weight has been an increase in eating disorders, especially in girls and young women. Young men also develop eating disorders, but they are only 5–10 percent of those affected. Women make up 90–95 percent. For that reason, people writing about eating disorders, unless they are writing specifically about boys and men, will talk about girls and women and use the pronoun "she."

Health professionals recognize three types of eating disorders. One is anorexia nervosa, in which a person has an irrational fear of getting fat and diets to the point of starvation. The second type of eating disorder is bulimia. A person eats large quantities of food and then makes herself throw up, takes laxatives, or uses other ways to avoid gaining weight. Third is compulsive eating, or binge eating. A compulsive eater eats large quantities of food, or binges, even when not physically hungry.

The American Anorexia Bulimia Association (AABA) states that more than five million Americans suffer from eating disorders. This number includes 5 percent of adolescent and adult women and 1 percent of men. The AABA also estimates that one thousand women die each year of anorexia. Other studies use percentages and say that 5–10 percent of long-term anoretics die of the disease. This means that anorexia has the highest death rate of all mental health illnesses.

By today's standards, extreme thinness is often viewed as attractive despite the harm that can result to mental and physical health.

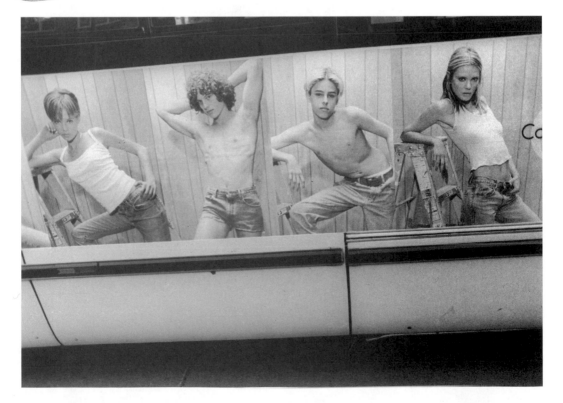

In 1994, for example, twenty-two-year-old gymnast Christy Henrich died of "multiple organ failure" caused by anorexia. She had begun dieting after being told by a judge at the 1989 World Championships that she'd never make the Olympics if she didn't lose weight. At that time she was four feet, eleven inches tall and weighed just ninety pounds. Her dieting developed into anorexia and bulimia, and in 1991 she had to withdraw from gymnastics because she was too frail. By 1993, the year before she died, she was down to sixty pounds.

Eating disorders now appear at younger ages. The average age of diagnosis used to be sixteen or seventeen. But it has dropped to fourteen for girls, and one study has shown that even fourth graders are "joining the diet craze and risk stunting their growth to maintain a very thin body."[2] Another survey found that of 2,379 nine- and ten-year-old girls, 40 percent said they were trying to lose weight. While some girls on diets are indeed overweight, others are yielding to societal pressures to be thin.

Pressure to be thin

Most experts believe these pressures are important reasons why so many girls develop eating disorders. Other reasons are found in the individual herself. These can include obsessive striving for perfection, low self-esteem, depression, conflicts over issues of control, family problems, discomfort with a changing body, uncertainty over society's views of women, and psychological or social traumas such as sexual abuse.

Kelli McNeill developed bulimia when she attended a highly competitive, private high school. She wrote this for *American Fitness* magazine:

> At the school I attend, [eating disorders] are the norm. To eat an entree at lunch would be scandalous. To go for second helpings would be anathema [horrible].
>
> Girls who are "normal" by national standards appear heavy and out of place at my school. A typical girl's weight is probably 10–15 pounds under the national averages. However, most of them still insist they are fat. Many girls who enroll as

new students eventually lose weight as well. In a recent survey, one in 13 girls was worried about a friend who might have an eating disorder. The first thing one senior girl noticed after transferring here from another school was how fanatical the girls are about exercising and not eating.

Self-starvation is an accepted social behavior.[3]

Kelli recovered from her eating disorder. But not everyone does.

Can anything be done to reverse this trend to be thinner and thinner? Many people hope that, by working together, teenagers, parents, teachers, and counselors can bring about healthier eating habits. But the first step is to understand what eating disorders are all about.

1

What Is an Eating Disorder?

KATHY WAS FOURTEEN years old when her family moved from New York to Ohio. She was a pretty girl with dark brown hair and matching eyes. Yet she was already troubled by family problems. Her father was cold and distant, and she didn't like the way he treated her mother.

Kathy hated her new school. She was highly intelligent, a top student who cared about her schoolwork. The kids here were different from the kids she had grown up with. They were rougher and less studious. She made some friends but still wasn't happy. She was even repelled by the way the girls "pigged out" at lunch time, "pushing mashed potatoes down their throats," she said to her mother. "Don't they care about how they look or what they're doing to themselves?"

It was then that Kathy decided to diet. Unlike the girls at school, she was going to look good. She wasn't overweight, but she wanted to be thinner. She would look perfect, like the superslim models that were starting to dominate fashion magazines. She continued to eat, but in small amounts. As she grew thinner, her menstrual periods became less frequent. At this point, her mother took her to a doctor. But the doctor only said, "It's just a phase she's going through. She'll get over it."

But Kathy didn't. "See, Mom, I'm fine," she said, and continued to diet. She grew thinner and more fragile, but remained a good student and graduated from high school

Sixties supermodel Twiggy is often said to have started the trend of ultrathin models. Many young girls compare themselves to models and shape their diet to achieve the greatest amount of weight loss.

with plans for college. However, when she told her college counselor that she wanted to become a physical therapist, he said, "You'll never make a physical therapist—you're too small and frail. Isn't there something else you could do?"

Kathy abandoned college until she could find something else. The following year, she met a young man and fell in love. Four months later, tragedy struck when the young man drowned in a boating accident. Despite counseling,

Kathy remained despondent and continued to diet. She would eat dinner with her family, but take little food and push it around her plate to look as if she were eating. Remaining thin was important. She later told a counselor that she liked the way superthin sixties model, Twiggy, looked.

A year later, when Kathy was twenty-one and weighed less than eighty pounds, she had a nervous breakdown. At the hospital, she was also diagnosed with anorexia. From then on, Kathy's life was a series of "recoveries" and relapses. By this time, she was also throwing up after eating.

Anorexia now controlled Kathy's life. It had started with a diet to be different from classmates she disliked. It continued as she faced tragedy and continued family problems. Between the ages of twenty-one and twenty-four she was in and out of hospitals and eating disorder centers. After one stay at a center in Chicago, she came home weighing seventy-nine pounds and feeling good. "She tried really hard," her mother says, but she relapsed again.

Finally, at age twenty-four, weighing just fifty pounds, Kathy became one of the 10 percent of anoretics who die of the disease. The official cause of death was heart failure, but "all of her internal organs were damaged,"[4] says her mother. Personal conflicts and problems had made it impossible to break the destructive eating patterns that dominated Kathy's short life.

Uncontrollable eating

Judith was a freshman at Harvard when she decided to improve her body along with her mind. Although an attractive five feet, seven inches tall, 130 pounds, she decided to lose fifteen pounds. "The same competitive, perfectionist drive that got me into Harvard fueled my dieting," she says. Her diet was extreme, about six hundred calories a day, and she exercised excessively. Soon she reached her goal—115 pounds.

But a week later, a piece of pizza led to a period of uncontrollable eating, also called compulsive eating or bingeing. Within six weeks she had gained back the fifteen pounds, plus ten more. A roller-coaster pattern began—strict dieting, followed by periods of bingeing. For a while, she dropped out of college because she was bingeing so much.

Sometimes she gave up on the dieting and resigned herself to being fat. Yet she never felt good about herself. "Whatever I accomplished—completing the [forty-five-hundred-mile cross-country] bike trip, graduating from college with honors, playing my flute in concert, winning writing awards—the bottom line was: I was fat. And as long as I was fat, I was a loser."

In her middle twenties, and tired of being fat, Judith joined a self-help organization for compulsive eaters. She began to understand that she turned to food when under pressure or when she was tired, angry, or lonely. But she still wanted to be thin. She went back to dieting and eventually started throwing up when she binged.

Finally, at the age of thirty-one, she entered an inpatient treatment center for bulimia and slowly began a path to recovery. Today, she realizes that it's okay to be imperfect, that she can get better without "getting every day exactly right."[5]

Dealing with problems

Zoe was a fifteen-year-old ballet dancer in Australia. Although already thin, she was told by her teacher that she had to lose more weight to be considered for a selective ballet school. When her weight was down to 78 percent of normal, her parents admitted her to a hospital, where she still refused to eat and gain weight. She was referred to eating disorder specialist and author Suzanne Abraham for treatment. When Abraham and her colleagues talked to Zoe, they learned about her fear of not being selected for the ballet school.

"We reassured her," says Abraham, "that in Australia, ballet dancers needed . . . [to be] . . . 80 to 90 percent of Average Body Weight, or they would 'not look good on stage.' Zoe accepted the reassurance and gained 5½ pounds in the next five weeks, which brought her weight into the desired range."[6] She was accepted into the ballet school. She has maintained an acceptable weight for dancers and enjoys the training she is receiving.

The stories of Kathy, Judith, and Zoe help explain what eating disorders are about. They are not just about losing weight. Kathy's diet began and continued as a way of dealing with problems she couldn't solve. Judith was driven to be perfect, and when she couldn't maintain her perfect diet, she saw herself as a failure and went the other way to

Staying thin is a way of life for dancers, which puts them at high risk for anorexia and bulimia.

bingeing. Zoe's dieting, on the other hand, never developed into an eating disorder even though she became too thin. Once convinced by trustworthy professionals that she could reach her goals at a higher weight, she was willing to eat enough to remove herself from the at-risk category.

Defining an eating disorder

What, then, is an eating disorder? "A person has an eating disorder when she uses food to work out her emotional problems," says Dr. Michael Maloney, a psychiatrist specializing in eating disorders and the author of *Straight Talk About Eating Disorders.* "Instead of feeling upset about a difficult situation, a person with an eating disorder tries to get rid of her feelings by eating or by dieting. . . . Food, weight, and dieting become ways to avoid all the other issues of [her] life."[7]

In many ways, adds Dr. Maloney, a person with an eating disorder becomes "addicted to food or dieting rather like an alcoholic is addicted to liquor or a drug addict to drugs. Instead of food being one part of her life, it becomes her whole life."[8]

Like Kathy and Judith, many girls with eating disorders start out trying to lose weight. But experts agree that weight is only part of the problem. College counselor Kathy Hotelling of Northern Illinois University in De Kalb says that many women who develop eating disorders feel overwhelmed by the many roles they are supposed to play. "They try to find something they can control in a world that seems increasingly uncontrollable," she explains, "and they turn to what they put in their mouths as something they can completely control."[9]

Anorexia nervosa

With her continuous dieting, Kathy developed the eating disorder called anorexia nervosa. The word anorexia means "loss of appetite," which is really not an anoretic's problem. Anoretics do have appetites and are hungry all the time. However, they work at controlling their hunger and fight not to give in to it.

Anoretics have a distorted body image and think they are fat even though they are dangerously thin.

A person is said to have anorexia when he or she has an irrational fear of getting fat and diets excessively. Anoretics have a distorted body image and think they're fat even though they're very thin. They continue to lose weight even when they are less than 85 percent of normal weight. A girl with anorexia who is five feet, six inches tall might weigh only 100 pounds, 20 percent less than a normal weight of 125 pounds, yet still feel "fat" and keep trying to lose more weight.

Some professionals today use a measurement called the Body Mass Index (BMI) as another way to describe anoretics. BMI is a ratio of height to weight. The most desirable BMI is between 19 and 24.9. Anoretics have a BMI of 17.5 or less. A one-hundred-pound person, five feet, six inches tall, would have a BMI of 16, considered to be severely underweight.

Anoretics also develop obsessive eating rituals, such as cutting food into a set number of pieces or measuring everything before eating tiny amounts. They often become obsessive about exercising as well. Girls stop getting monthly menstrual periods, or if younger, never start.

Cherry Boone O'Neill, daughter of fifties singing star Pat Boone, writes of her long struggle with both anorexia and bulimia in *Starving for Attention,* a struggle that began with a strict diet at age thirteen. In talking about her teen years, she tells about her obsession with food and exercise:

> My entire existence seemed to revolve around my mandatory four hours of exercise while most of my thoughts gravitated toward menus, recipes, and caloric computations. What was left of my resources was reserved for schoolwork and performing. Leisure time was usually spent copying recipe ideas from magazines and newspapers. I still got straight A's and even while traveling weeks at a time [Cherry regularly performed with her parents and three sisters] I maintained my rigorous schedule of jogging, stretching, calisthenics, and swimming.
>
> I was never without a specific dietary plan, whether based on daily caloric intake or the latest reducing fad. . . . Rigid regimentation had taken over my life. Any disturbance of my painstakingly structured personal agenda was like yanking on a tightly held security blanket. I regarded phone calls from my closest friends as unforgivable interruptions.[10]

Unlike Kathy, Cherry recovered from her eating disorders. She later used her celebrity status to make others aware of these dangerous illnesses.

Who develops anorexia

As with Kathy and Cherry O'Neill, the typical age for becoming anorexic is the early to middle teens, a time of great change. There are new conflicts with parents, a desire for independence, attention—or lack of it—from the opposite sex, and new challenges at school. There is also puberty, when girls' bodies develop breasts and hips—and fat. These physical changes are normal and necessary for reproduction. But they don't fit the "ideal" body that girls see on TV or in magazines.

Girls who develop anorexia are usually white and middle-to-upper class. This isn't surprising, since studies show that white girls and women are more likely to be unhappy with their bodies than African Americans. However, studies over the past ten years have shown that anorexia is increasing among other races and cultures, too. No one, it seems, is immune to the quest to be thin.

Anoretics are often model children from families with high expectations. They excel in school and other activities and are eager to please their parents and teachers. They have been called "perfect little girls." But there is another side to their lives.

"Many people with anorexia and bulimia have in common a low self-esteem and a cruel perfectionism that allow them no flaws in appearance or performance of any activity undertaken," writes Kaz Cook, author of *Real Gorgeous: The Truth About Body and Beauty*.[11]

At some point in their struggle to reduce, they develop a distorted body image, insisting they are fat, even when they obviously look as if they are starving. Tina Lauer is a good example. She is twenty-nine, no longer a teen, but she has been struggling with anorexia and bulimia since she was fifteen. When featured on CNN's documentary show IMPACT, she weighed seventy-five pounds and looked as thin as a "walking skeleton."[12] Yet she still said she felt fat.

"Every time I look in the mirror, I see an obese person who should be on a diet, and should not be gaining weight," she said. "I already felt obese when I came in here [at sixty-three pounds], and now I feel even worse. My clothes are starting to get tight in the waist."[13]

Losing control

Even if they want to eat, some anoretics can't bring themselves to break their self-imposed program of discipline. Many others, however, can't always stick to the rigid diet-and-exercise regimen they have set up for themselves. Marya Hornbacher writes in her book, *Wasted: A Memoir of Anorexia and Bulimia*, "Sometimes you break down. The body and the soul protest deprivation. We [at boarding school] broke down from time to time, ordered pizzas or subs, sat in the main room of the dorm in front of the television, eating."[14]

Then, in an effort to undo the "damage," anoretics will purge what they ate through the use of forced vomiting, laxatives, diuretics (pills that help the body lose water), or excessive exercise. At that point, they have developed bulimia as well, the most common eating disorder.

Bulimia

The word bulimia comes from two Greek words: *bous,* which means ox, and *limos,* which means hunger. Thus, to be bulimic literally means to feel the hunger of an ox.

About 40–50 percent of anoretics become bulimic, but not all people with bulimia have anorexia. Many, like Judith, maintain a normal body weight or are overweight. Their disease is not as noticeable as the anoretic's and can go undetected for years. Several years ago, movie actress and fitness promoter Jane Fonda surprised the world when she stated that she suffered from bulimia from the time she was twelve until she was thirty-five.

A person is said to have bulimia when he or she binges repeatedly by eating enormous quantities of food at one sitting, and then purges regularly through vomiting and/or the use of diuretics or laxatives. Some bulimics try to eliminate the calories through strict dieting, fasting, or vigorous exercise. Medically, to be diagnosed bulimic, a person must binge and then engage in weight-prevention measures at least twice a week for at least three months. A person with bulimia feels a lack of control during the binges and sometimes shows other compulsive behaviors, such as drug abuse or shoplifting. Male bulimics are more likely to exercise compulsively as a way to get rid of calories.

Like people with anorexia, bulimics are trying to be perfect. They want to appear competent and successful to the world. However, they are hiding a low level self-esteem and are often depressed. When they feel anxious and unsure of themselves, they turn to food—and lots of it.

How much is a lot? An article in *FDA Consumer* describes it this way:

> While normal food intake for a teenager is 2,000 to 3,000 calories in a day, bulimic binges average about 3,400 calories in 1¼ hours, according to one study. Some bulimics consume up to 20,000 calories in binges lasting as long as eight hours. Some spend $50 or more a day on food and may resort to stealing food or money to support their obsession.[15]

Bulimia in college

While anorexia starts in the early teens, bulimia usually starts later. One of the most common times is when a girl goes off to college—another time of great change. She is leaving home for the first time and facing new experiences. Often, she's not sure if she'll succeed. In addition, food is constantly available and there's no "mom" around to see that she chooses healthy meals and snacks. Overeating can be a way of coping. But then comes the fear of becoming overweight. For some girls, the solution is strict weight control—first dieting and then bingeing and purging when the desire to eat becomes overwhelming.

"What turns bulimia into an epidemic [in colleges] is that it's often a behavior that friends teach each other," writes Leslie Morgan in *Seventeen*. "And the relative anonymity of college creates a hospitable environment for the disease."[16]

Some studies show that close to 30 percent of college women have signs of bulimia. "When I make a presentation to a group of women, I no longer ask, 'Who knows someone with an eating disorder?' I ask, 'Who doesn't?'"[17] says Julie Campbell-Ruggaard, a member of the Student Counseling Service at Miami University in Oxford, Ohio.

Rooming with others who are bingeing and purging makes it easier for girls to accept that behavior. Susan Klebanoff, a clinical psychologist and associate of the Eating Disorder Resource Center in New York City, suspects that when women binge and purge together, there is less conscious shame because the entire group participates in the abnormal behavior. "They tend to think if so-and-so is doing it, then it's OK for me,"[18] she says.

Campbell-Ruggaard tells of one student who told her sorority that she had an eating disorder. The girl said that it was "agony" for her to attend events where food was served. Six or seven sorority sisters admitted to the same problem. So they made a pact. "They would all sit together at functions, eating the Doritos cheese dip, with the tacit understanding that they'd slip away and purge."[19]

People with bulimia think they are controlling their weight and therefore their lives, but bulimia can take on a life of its own. It becomes obsessive behavior, and the person finds she can't stop the bingeing and purging, even when she wants to do so.

The pressure of leaving home and going to college pushes some young women into a cycle of bingeing and purging.

Compulsive eating, or binge eating

It may seem odd with all the emphasis on being thin, but more people in the United States are overweight than ever before. Twenty-two percent of teenagers are overweight, up from 15 percent less than thirty years ago, and 12 percent are so overweight that their health is affected. In addition, 35 percent of American women are considered to be overweight.

Seda Ebrahimi, director of the Eating Disorders Treatment Program at McLean Hospital in Belmont, Massachusetts, says that one-third of obese patients may be binge eaters. Like bulimics, binge eaters find comfort in food and turn to it when they feel anxious or upset. Unlike bulimics, however, they don't purge. According to Dr. Ebrahimi, this lack of purging makes the illness seem less severe, causing many health professionals to think the patient is merely overeating. The binge eating is then treated as a dietary problem instead of a psychiatric disorder.

But Dr. Ebrahimi believes that the possibility the patient has an eating disorder should not be overlooked. "Binge eating is an avoidance coping mechanism," he says. "During the binge, the person 'mentally and emotionally checks out' and is unable to stop the out-of-control eating." [20]

A person is said to be a compulsive eater or binge eater when he or she continues to eat even when not hungry, often turning to food when feeling anxious or in need of comfort. A compulsive eater has repeated episodes of bingeing and feels out of control when bingeing. He or she often feels shame or disgust afterwards, seeing in the overeating a lack of will power.

Many compulsive eaters also follow a pattern of dieting, followed by bingeing, so they are not always obese.

Why overeat?

As with anorexia and bulimia, the causes of binge eating are many, and often unclear. Some people have suggested, however, that overeating in girls is a response to special pressures on young women in our society. In her book, *Reviving Ophelia,* psychologist Mary Pipher talks about teenage girls:

They are coming of age in a more dangerous, sexualized and media-saturated culture. They face incredible pressures to be beautiful and sophisticated, which in junior high means using chemicals and being sexual. As they navigate a more danger-ous world, girls are less protected.[21]

Some young women, Pipher says, use food to get rid of their emotional pain. When they gain weight and become "fat," they feel even worse because it's impossible to be heavy in America and still feel good about yourself. She says:

They diet and feel miserable, then they eat and feel better, but meanwhile their dieting makes their metabolism grow more and more sluggish. Over time weight loss becomes associated with control, and weight gain with out-of-control behavior. They become more obsessed with calories and weight. Soon it's not just their eating but their lives that are out of control.[22]

"Never be too thin"

There's an old saying, "You can never be too thin or too rich." But more people are beginning to question the idea that if thin is good, thinner is better. Some doctors are try-ing to help their patients understand that people have dif-ferent metabolisms; that is, their bodies use up calories at different rates. Some fashion designers, too, as well as magazines and retail stores, are beginning to recognize that people who buy clothes come in all shapes and sizes.

But still, the desire to be thin is very powerful in Amer-ica today, and the pressure can be found all around us.

2

The Pressure
to Be Thin

TEENAGERS TODAY ARE surrounded by images of slenderness. They turn on the television or pick up magazines and see beautiful people who are also thin. The diet industry is a $40 billion business and growing. Magazines are filled with articles on counting calories and losing weight, not to mention advertisements glorifying thin bodies.

Both boys and girls feel society's pressures to have perfect bodies. But there is a difference. Boys are given more leeway in how they look. They are taught to value their bodies for what they can do and themselves for what they can achieve. Not that boys are problem free. They can develop eating disorders when they try to mold their bodies to reach a specific sports ideal. In addition, men today are expected to be slimmer, more muscular, and more youthful. And like women, increasing numbers of young men are developing eating disorders.

But girls are more constrained. Stephen Bailey, associate professor of anthropology at Tufts University in Boston, says,

> Men have a greater range of weights and physiques they can feel comfortable with, while women have a specific physique to strive for. These days, for women, it's a weird combination of muscularity, slenderness, and large breasts—which no woman can possibly achieve.[23]

Yet girls and women do try to achieve this ideal. They have been taught that their bodies—and often they themselves—

are valued for how they look. As Mary Pipher says in *Reviving Ophelia,*

> Beauty is the defining characteristic for American women. It's the necessary and often sufficient condition for social success. It is important for women of all ages, but the pressure to be beautiful is most intense in early adolescence. Girls worry about their clothes, makeup, skin and hair. But most of all they worry about their weight. Peers place an enormous value on thinness.[24]

Ideals of beauty

Slim, young women dominate popular TV shows like *Beverly Hills, 90210.* Even though one study found that most girls believe TV's female characters are "unrealistically thin," it's hard for teenage girls to resist the message. "All the attractive women on TV and in the movies are skinny," says fourteen-year-old Rona Luo, a New York high school student. "It's not so easy to hold out and think, 'I'm going to be who I am.'"[25]

Television and magazine ads often portray extreme thinness as desirable.

Trendy ads, such as those for Calvin Klein jeans, also feature superthin models. British model Kate Moss, for example, is five feet, seven inches tall and weighs just 100 pounds, well below her ideal weight of about 135 pounds. With a BMI of 16, she is considered severely underweight. In fact, people have sometimes written "Feed me" across her image on ad posters.

Miss America contestants, too, have fallen below healthy weights for adult women. In fact, one study concluded that 60 percent of Miss America contestants weighed at least 15 percent less than their healthy weight, which means, wrote one researcher, that "a majority of these 'ideals' of our society may be classified as having one of the major symptoms of an eating disorder."[26]

The late Princess Diana stated as early as 1992 that she suffered from bulimia. Yet she was considered to be an ideal beauty. Her then sister-in-law, Sarah Ferguson, duchess of

Stung by comments about her weight, Sarah Ferguson joined Weight Watchers and now maintains a healthy, ideal body weight.

York, was not so fortunate. When she gained weight, she was ridiculed in the press as "The Duchess of Pork." Now a spokesperson for Weight Watchers, Fergie tries to stay between 131 and 158 pounds, a healthy weight for her five feet, seven and one-half inches.

Focus on weight

Another problem for teenagers trying to find their identities is that the culture often focuses on women's weight, rather than their talents. For example, *Titanic* star Kate

Winslet is a talented actress who was nominated for an Academy Award. At age twenty-two she has, in the words of writer Jacquelyn Mitchard, "the slim, healthy, curvy, utterly gorgeous young woman's body. . . . At 5 feet 6 or 7, she weighs 130 pounds."[27]

This is a healthy weight, but Winslet is definitely not skinny. Most models and young actresses are fragile in comparison, and for a while Winslet's weight was much discussed.

Thin equals success

Teenage girls see these "thin" messages at a time when their own bodies are changing. They are developing hips and breasts, which means an increase in fat. All of this is normal. Yet girls today are not only presented with a thin body as the ideal, they are even being told that everyone can—or should—achieve that goal.

"I WANT TO BE THIN LIKE ALLY M⁺BEAL, STACKED LIKE BARBIE and ETERNALLY YOUNG LIKE A SUPERMODEL.... NOW IF YOU'LL EXCUSE ME, I HAVE TO GO VOMIT MY HAPPY MEAL."

In an article in *Glamour,* Judith Rodin writes,

> We've come to believe . . . that everyone who works out can achieve the lean, healthy-looking ideal, provided that she puts enough time and effort into it. We've been led to believe that we can control more than we actually can. . . . Being thin and fit is now a metaphor for success.[28]

Some feminists take Rodin's position even further. For example, Susie Orbach says in her new edition of *Fat Is a Feminist Issue:*

> We live in a culture that . . . sees fatness and thinness as ultimate statements about people's worth. . . . The current aesthetic of thinness forces cruel pressures on the individual women. Few women are naturally thin, or indeed naturally any size. We are a variety of sizes. But the thin aesthetic which has dominated the last twenty years has put women in the impossible position of feeling that they must curb their appetites and their food intake.[29]

A feminist view

Body types go in and out of fashion. In the nineteenth century, for example, women were expected to be round. At a time when many people did not have enough to eat, being plump was a symbol of wealth. Today, however, with food plentiful in the United States, successful people are thin.

Some people believe that thinness is valued because men are, by nature, thinner than women. In their book, *Overcoming Overeating,* Jane Hirschmann and Carol Munter point out that men are "thinner, harder, and more muscular than the female, who is rounded and curved by fat deposits on breasts and hips."[30] They maintain that women strive to be thin in order to be more like men, who still have more power and control than women. That is, ambitious women may seek to gain power by cultivating a resemblance to those now in control.

Writer Naomi Wolf sees keeping women thin as a way to keep them passive and powerless. In her best-seller, *The Beauty Myth,* she cites researchers S. C. Wooley and O. W. Wooley, who "confirmed what most women know too well—that concern with weight leads to a 'virtual collapse of self-esteem and sense of effectiveness.'"[31]

Wolf also quotes researchers J. Polivy and C. P. Herman, who found that long-term limiting of food intake leads to personality traits of "passivity, anxiety and emotionality."[32] These characteristics, she says, and not the thinness itself, are what some elements of American society want in women today. In other words, constant dieting and concentrating on being thin keep a woman focused on her body and its faults. This negative outlook, in turn, generates low self-esteem, and such a woman is less ambitious and less threatening.

Impact on teens

No matter what the reason, young women today feel an intense pressure to be thin. It is no surprise, therefore, that study after study shows that most girls are unhappy with their bodies and are willing to deprive themselves of food to meet the culture's standards. The national organization, Eating Disorders Awareness and Prevention (EDAP), states that 20–30 percent of girls in the fourth to sixth grades think they should be thinner, and 30–50 percent of girls aged twelve to fourteen say that they are concerned about being fat. Some of these girls undoubtedly are overweight, but others are simply responding to pressures to be thin.

For example, Sandra Arbetter reports in *Current Health 2* that the University of South Carolina studied more than three thousand fifth to eighth graders. They found out that more than 40 percent said they felt fat or wanted to lose weight, while only 20 percent were really overweight.

Another survey of eleven thousand high school students was conducted by the Centers for Disease Control and Prevention. They learned that almost half of the girls were dieting, even though many didn't think they were overweight.

The dark side of being thin

What teenagers don't see, however, is that many "ideal" beauties use less than ideal ways to keep their weight down.

Christine Alt, for example, wanted to please her family by being as successful as her sister, supermodel Carol Alt.

But to be a fashion model, she had to lose weight. At first she tried a moderate diet, but didn't see much progress. So she started to eat less and less and exercise more. At one point, she exercised three hours a day and went ten days without eating—living on seltzer water.

She talks about her anorexia in a 1992 *Glamour* article:

> I know it's hard to believe—why would anyone do this? But when you start losing so much weight, you don't know what's normal anymore. I remember seeing Karen Carpenter on the

Singer Karen Carpenter (pictured with her brother) did not recover from her seven-year battle with anorexia. She died at the age of thirty-two.

cover of *People* after she died from anorexia. All I could think about was how lucky she was she died so skinny—and could I get that skinny *without* dying?

During this time I would go to the agency to be weighed. I remember once I was wearing a sweater and wool pants, and I came out 115 pounds—size four. I'm five feet eleven, and a little tall for a four! But they just told me to keep going: "You're doing great on your diet!" It seemed that as long as clients booked me, they didn't care how I lost the weight. But that was the funny thing: Clients didn't book me much—because thanks to all the dieting, I had no personality. My eyes, my hair, my body—*everything*—looked dead.[33]

Christine Alt recovered from her anorexia and bulimia, and now models size-twelve clothing. But although she is eating normally, she has intestinal damage and wonders if she'll be able to have children.

Other celebrities

Christine Alt is just one example of celebrities who suffered from eating disorders. Elton John has said that he was bulimic for six years; Academy Award winning actress Sally Field says that when she was twenty, she began three years of starving, bingeing, and taking diet pills; and singer Paula Abdul has had problems with bingeing.

Eating disorders can start very young. Tracey Gold, who played the daughter in the sitcom *Growing Pains,* became anorexic at the age of twelve. She seemed to recover, but at nineteen she began dieting again when a casting director teased her about her weight. At five feet, three and one-half inches tall and weighing 133 pounds, she decided to lose twenty pounds. She was so delighted with all the praise she received for losing weight, she continued to diet. When her weight reached 90 pounds, she had to leave the show to go into the hospital. At one point in 1992, she weighed as little as 80 pounds.

Then one day Tracey looked in the mirror and realized she could actually die. That was the beginning of her recovery. In 1994, weighing ninety-five pounds, she got married. Three years later, she had a healthy baby boy.

There are more examples. Models and ballerinas have been particularly vulnerable. In her autobiography, *Dancing on My Grave,* former ballerina Gelsey Kirkland reports that the head of her ballet troupe once stopped a class, thumped on the bones of Kirkland's chest, and said, "Must see the bones. Eat nothing." [34] At the time, she weighed less than one hundred pounds.

Eating disorders in athletes

Even athletes, who understand the importance of strong, healthy bodies, are not immune from eating disorders. Eating disorders are increasing in athletes, especially in sports such as gymnastics and figure skating, where participants are judged on technical and artistic merit. In fact, a 1992 American College of Sports Medicine study found that eating disorders affected 62 percent of females in sports like figure skating and gymnastics.

Eating disorders occur in male athletes, too. When boys are involved in sports that require weight limitations—wrestlers, swimmers, runners and jockeys—they, too, show an increase in disordered eating. Dr. Arnold E. Andersen, a professor of psychiatry at the University of Iowa College of Medicine and one of the country's leading researchers in eating disorders, sees this as suggesting that "behavioral reinforcement, not gender, is the crucial element." [35]

Yet the pressure has always been greatest on females. Cathy Rigby, a 1972 Olympic gymnast, struggled with anorexia and bulimia for twelve years and went into cardiac arrest twice because of it. Nadia Comaneci, the popular 1976 Olympic gold medalist gymnast, has also admitted to problems with eating disorders.

In fairness to these and other sports, however, it must also be stated that at least one study of female college athletes, reported in the *International Journal of Sports Nutrition,* concluded that the disposition to eating disorders in athletes might have more to do with a striving for high achievement and perfection than with the sports themselves. More research will undoubtedly be done on this controversial subject.

Thinner and thinner

It is clear, however, that gymnasts—and figure skaters, too—have become thinner over the past twenty years. Consider this, as reported by Joan Ryan in *Little Girls in Pretty Boxes:*

> In 1976 the six [female] U.S. Olympic gymnasts were, on average, seventeen and a half years old, stood 5 feet 3½ inches and weighed 106 pounds. By the 1992 Olympics in Barcelona, the average U.S. Olympic gymnast was sixteen years old, stood 4 feet 9 inches and weighed 83 pounds—a year younger, 6½ inches shorter and 23 pounds lighter than her counterpart of sixteen years before.[36]

A similar trend to younger stars with thinner bodies can be seen in ladies figure skating, too. Peggy Fleming was nineteen years old when she won the Olympic gold medal in 1968, Dorothy Hamill was nineteen in 1976, Katerina Witt was eighteen in 1984 and twenty-two in 1988. Contrast this with 1998's gold medalist, Tara Lapinsky, whose slim fifteen-year-old body wowed the world with extraordinary jumps.

Weight limitations in such sports as wrestling, swimming, and running have caused some male athletes to suffer from eating disorders.

A trend of younger, thinner bodies is evident in ladies figure skating. Tara Lapinsky (pictured) was only fifteen years old when she won the 1998 Olympic gold medal.

These two sports illustrate the contradiction of modern womanhood, says Ryan:

Society has allowed women to aspire higher, but to do so a woman must often reject that which makes her female, including motherhood. Similarly, gymnastics and figure skating remove the limits of a girl's body, teaching it to soar beyond what seems possible. Yet they also imprison it, binding it like the tiny Victorian waist or the Chinese woman's foot. The girls aren't allowed passage into adulthood. To survive in the sports, they beat back puberty, desperate to stay small and thin, refusing to let their bodies grow up. . . . The physical skills have become so demanding that only a body shaped like a missile—in other words, a body shaped like a boy's— can excel. Breasts and hips slow the spins, lower the leaps and disrupt the clean, lean body lines the judges reward. "Women's gymnastics" and "ladies figure skating" are mis- nomers today. Once the athletes become women, their elite careers wither.[37]

Such restrictions are not as evident in sports such as ten- nis, basketball, and soccer, where performance and scoring are not dependent on appearance. But they do appear in track and field, where female curves can slow perfor- mance. As one high jumper at the University of Texas put it, "No one in track wants boobs."[38]

Sometimes fashion doesn't want female curves either. Katie Ford, CEO of the famous Ford Models agency, sees the current "look" desired by photographers and maga- zines as being "slender and flat chested. . . . New models tend to be young—15, 16—because that's the only time of your life you have that kind of body."[39]

A clear message

To a young teen, the message is clear. A maturing body with feminine curves is not to be welcomed. It is to be fought.

Marya Hornbacher, who suffered from both anorexia and bulimia during her teenage years, writes,

> When a prepubescent shape is held up as an ideal [to girls go- ing through puberty], they may balk at their own bodies' sud- den mute refusal to adhere to cultural requirements. They might, if their personal chemistry is right, go head-to-head with nature . . . in a campaign to defeat their own biology.[40]

William N. Davis, executive director of The Renfrew Foundation in Philadelphia, an eating disorders treatment center, describes who is most susceptible:

The vulnerable ones—those who are struggling with feelings of inadequacy, loneliness or abuse—are most prone to turn to eating disorders because our culture proclaims that thinness can help them, soothe them, and make it all better.[41]

It is only after they are caught in the grips of an eating disorder that they realize the culture was wrong. Being thin does not solve their problems—and an eating disorder just adds to them.

3

Other Causes of Eating Disorders

NOT EVERY TEENAGE girl develops an eating disorder. In fact, most do not, even if they are dissatisfied with their bodies. Similarly, most girls—and boys—who go on diets do not develop eating disorders. The pressure to be thin may be why some teens choose food as a way of dealing with problems, but those who develop eating disorders are responding to a combination of troubling factors in their lives.

The drive to be perfect

Many teens who develop anorexia feel that they must be perfect in all that they do. Dr. Raymond Vath, the psychiatrist who treated Cherry Boone O'Neill, says, "The anoretic maintains ideals and behavioral goals that are absolutely above reproach in order to avoid punishment or rejection. There is frequently a frantic striving to achieve, motivated by underlying guilt and remorse for failing to live up to expectations."[42]

Other researchers refer to anoretics as "model children," who try to meet the high standards that their parents and others expect. They are intense and do other things to excess as well. Bulimics often exhibit behaviors such as drug abuse or shoplifting.

Marya Hornbacher describes the personality of an eating-disordered person as "extreme . . . highly competitive, incredibly self-critical, driven, perfectionistic, tending toward excess."[43] Cherry Boone O'Neill refers to herself as a perfectionist. It was part of her performing, her schoolwork, and finally, her dieting. When she lost weight successfully, it was still not enough. She discovered her mother's diet pills and began using them to suppress her appetite and give her extra energy.

Control issues

Why are some teenagers so driven to perfection? High family expectations to achieve are often at the root of unrealistic goals. Such families can also be controlling, expecting everything from grades to appearance to behavior to be perfect. Some teens who fail to live up to these expectations starve themselves as a form of punishment. Others turn to food as a way of controlling some part of their lives: no one can make them eat, and no one can keep them from throwing up. Food becomes their source of power.

One girl recovering from bulimia says, "I thought if I could starve myself, I could do anything. Bingeing was a way of stuffing all my bad feelings inside, and then throwing them up and getting rid of them—for a little while." Like many teens, she felt her parents were too controlling. "I thought that perfect was the only way to be,"[44] she says.

Another girl, who first started dieting in fifth grade, put herself on an all liquid diet. "I was awesome," she says. "I liked them watching me make drinks. I felt like they couldn't stop me. I had a whole lot of power over everyone."[45] Her dieting grew out-of-control, however, and she developed an eating disorder.

Trying to control or repress emotions can also be a factor in eating disorders. Some families do not talk about feelings or problems. Girls, especially, are often expected to keep anger or aggression inside, while considering the feelings of others. Many are raised to please others and to look to others for approval. But feelings cannot be suppressed indefinitely. If teens are sad, lonely, or uncertain, and don't feel they can express their feelings, they may use food as a way to find comfort—and then use purging as a way to get rid of the food and the feelings.

Low self-esteem and depression

Experts agree that anoretics and bulimics suffer from low self-esteem and often depression. Some may feel unworthy because they fail to live up to some perfect ideal. Others might have a genetic tendency toward depression. And for girls, entering adolescence often brings with it a drop in self-esteem.

In their efforts to measure up to a perfect ideal, anoretics and bulimics experience crushing depression and low self-esteem.

Jane E. Brody of the *New York Times* reports on studies by the American Association of University Women and the Commonwealth Fund, a New York–based women's health organization. Their studies document "that more often than not, girls entering puberty experience a crisis in confidence that renders them vulnerable to risky health behaviors that they may not have the strength or will to resist."[46]

The Commonwealth Fund study further shows that the older the teenage girl, the lower the self-esteem. By contrast, boys' self-esteem increases as they grow older, and more than half of high school boys had feelings of high self-confidence.

Psychologist Emily Hancock, author of *The Girl Within,* cites these studies and her own research. Girls' self-esteem peaks at age nine, she says, then begins to sink. They slowly lose their "strength, independence, and lucidity and become riveted to the issue of how they look." They feel they can't measure up to the images of beauty—thin, waiflike—and "many fall into depression, eating disorders and drug abuse."[47]

Depression is closely associated with low self-esteem, reports Brody. The Commonwealth Fund study found that 29 percent of girls said they had suicidal thoughts, 27 percent said they often felt sad, and 33 percent of older girls said they felt like crying "many days" or "every day." When stressed, they often turned to cigarettes, alcohol, and drugs. Feelings of hopelessness and despair also made them more vulnerable to society's message to be thin—and therefore more vulnerable to eating disorders.

Biological and genetic factors

Many researchers today also recognize that chemical imbalances in the brain may contribute to the development and persistence of eating disorders. Dr. Timothy Walsh, who oversees the eating disorders clinic at the New York Psychiatric Institute, said on CNN's IMPACT, "My belief is that anorexia nervosa, at its root, includes a problem with brain chemistry. My hunch is some of these chemical changes help explain why the disorder, once established, is so persistent."[48]

Neurochemical imbalances, for example, are among the factors causing depression, anxiety, obsessive-compulsive behavior, and bipolar disorder (cycles of periods of hyper-activity followed by depression). Depression—along with compulsive behavior—is particularly associated with bulimia, and antidepressant medication is now used in treatment.

Eating disorders tend to run in families, often appearing in families which have a higher than usual incidence of depression or substance abuse. Studies of twins have shown that if one twin has an eating disorder—or depression, or other mental illness—the other is likely to as well, says Dr. Joanne Witkowski, chief of the Department of Psychiatry at Kaiser-Permanente Medical Center in Riverside, California, and co-chair of the Eating Disorder Task Force of the Southern California Permanente Medical Group. "We all have genes that give us certain tendencies," she says. "That's why some people are more prone to heart disease and diabetes."[49] That's also why some may be more prone to eating disorders.

Sexual abuse or other trauma

Many young women with eating disorders have something else in common—they use food as a way to cope with some form of abuse or trauma. "Between twenty percent and fifty percent of women with eating disorders are survivors of sexual abuse as children or adults," says clinical psychologist Elizabeth Wheeler, director of the eating disorders program at the University of Massachusetts Medical Center in Worcester. "It starts as a smart strategy, a reasonable response to pain. They use food to numb powerful emotions."[50]

A study at a residential treatment center in Philadelphia for women with eating disorders, reported in *Seventeen* magazine, showed that more than 60 percent of patients said they had been sexually abused at one time in their lives. But abuse can take other forms, as well. It can be physical abuse or emotional abuse, such as threats, insults, belittling, or even emotional indifference.

Teens who have been abused are more likely to accept society's views of beauty and worth. They use food to deal with their pain. They may binge because food brings them comfort. Many say that food is the only thing that is "always there for them. Food does not yell at them, hurt them and will never leave them."[51] Purging can be a way of releasing emotions, of getting feelings out. Many bulimics report a feeling of calm after purging.

Sometimes victims of sexual abuse will overeat or stop eating, thinking that if they are too fat or too thin, they will be unattractive to the abuser and will be left alone. Like other girls who develop eating disorders, many abuse victims seize on food as a means of control. Feeling that they have no control over the abuse, they can at least control the food that goes in and out of their bodies. Recovery can be especially difficult for abuse victims because the eating disorder has been their way of coping with the trauma. Without the eating disorder, they have to find another way of dealing with what happened to them.

To a young girl who suffers abuse or trauma, food may be a means of control and purging a way of releasing emotions.

Cosmopolitan magazine tells the story of Marianne, now nineteen, who developed anorexia when she was sixteen as a response to the self-hatred she felt from the physical and emotional abuse of her father:

> "I thought my body was evil," she says. "I'd been told that I was a mistake. My father slapped me across the face, threw me against the wall, said I was ugly, that I never should have been born."

> During high school, Marianne slipped below 70 pounds and was hospitalized. Now she's in outpatient therapy and back to normal weight, but she struggles every day. "Sometimes life gets real hard, and I'm tempted to start fasting again," she admits sadly.[52]

Confusion over their roles as women

Some girls develop eating disorders as a response to the many mixed messages they get about their roles as women. Advertisements urge them to be sexy, but if they act on their sexuality, they are called sluts. Parents and schools want them to be smart, but their peers may reject them for being overly studious. With these often conflicting messages, it is sometimes easier to narrow them all down to one: be thin.

In their book, *The Cost of Competence,* researchers Brett Silverstein and Deborah Perlick talk about gender identity. They state that crucial questions for all people are, "Who am I? Where do I fit in? Am I valued?"[53] Belonging to any group that is considered inferior can cause ambivalence, or uncertainty, about who they are and how they feel about themselves. This ambivalence can cause low self-esteem, depression and a poor body image.

Silverstein and Perlick also found that symptoms for women increase during periods of changing gender roles. Thus today, girls who have been brought up to value and strive for achievement in nontraditional fields may develop depression and disordered eating when they confront biases against women in those areas. This argument is supported by evidence that women with eating disorders are often highly motivated and achievement oriented.

Moderate exercise and a healthy diet is a way to maintain an ideal weight.

Family stress, alcoholism, substance abuse

Eating disorders often develop at times of great family stress, such as divorce. One former anoretic, whose parents divorced when she was three, said,

> Confused and hurt by the divorce, I felt that I had to be perfect to make things easier for my family. As far back as third grade, I stayed up late doing homework while my siblings slept. I cleaned obsessively. . . . But no matter how much I tried to make myself and the world around me perfect, I felt that I fell short.[54]

Sometimes, too, parents going through a divorce are so wrapped up in their own problems, they have nothing left to give to their children. A teen may turn to food as a substitute—or may be more easily influenced by messages to be thin. Alcoholism, substance abuse, or other stresses on a family can have a similar effect on teens trying to find their place in the world.

Feelings of worthlessness

Peggy Claude-Pierre, who runs the well-publicized, and sometimes controversial, Montreux Clinic for eating disorders in Canada, has her own theory about eating disorders. She believes they are caused by what she calls a confirmed negativity condition, or CNC. By this she means that people with eating disorders, both male and female, believe that they are "bad" and don't deserve to live. Claude-Pierre recalls a conversation with her younger daughter:

"Honey, [what makes you think you're] so bad?" I asked.

"You don't understand. I just am."

"What have you ever done that's so bad? You've been such a good girl all your life—a wonderful child."

"I don't know the answer," she replied, "but I know it's in my head all the time."[55]

According to Claude-Pierre, this negative idea comes from an inborn supersensitivity. People with CNC have a great sense of responsibility and feel that it is up to them to make things "right," whether in their families or in the wider world. When they can't, they feel weak and unworthy of living. Not everyone who appears to exhibit CNC will develop an eating disorder, but if exposed to the right triggers, such as illness, divorce, or other family problems, the negative mind can take control and tell the person he or she doesn't deserve to eat.

Strict dieting

People who severely restrict their intake of food are also considered to be at high risk for developing eating disorders. According to Naomi Wolf in *The Beauty Myth,* dieting women often restrict their calories to a level that borders on semistarvation. Studies have shown that semistarvation, whether caused by scarcity or dieting, can lead to irritability, depression, anxiety, and poor concentration.

In a study at the University of Minnesota to learn the effects of starvation, thirty-six healthy, young, male volunteers were put on a long-term, low-calorie diet. Their food intake was reduced by half. Wolf maintains that this 50 percent reduction is a typical dieting technique used by women.

Weight-Loss Methods Used by Females

	percent using	
	age 10–14	age 15–25
Avoiding eating between meals	73	78
Exercising (usually alone)	44	75
Dieting—"own diet"	35	55
Avoiding eating breakfast	—	48
Keeping busy to avoid temptation to eat	38	46
Selecting low-calorie foods	32	41
Counting calories	—	34
Avoiding situations where food is offered	15	25
Dieting with a friend	—	22
Using illness as an excuse not to eat	—	21
Exercising with a friend	—	20
Drinking water before eating	29	18
Taking "natural" laxatives	11	16
Lying about the amount of food eaten	—	16
Weighing self several times a day	4	15
Smoking cigarettes	2	14
Dieting—magazine diet	16	12
Keeping refrigerator or cupboards empty	—	12
Avoiding eating with family	1	10

Survey of 300 female teenagers age 10–14 and 106 healthy women age 15–25.

Source: *Eating Disorders: The Facts.* New York: Oxford University Press, 4th ed., 1977.

After the men lost 25 percent of their weight, the study noted effects of semistarvation. They became depressed, anxious and often unable to function normally at work. In addition, they began to obsess about food. Some would binge and purge—some felt hungry even after eating large meals. When they returned to a normal diet and began to gain weight, some men were concerned about feeling fat. Yet all of these men were considered mentally healthy and emotionally stable before the study began. This study is important because it shows that some characteristics of eating disorders can actually be caused by semistarvation. Eating healthy foods in adequate amounts can help a teen avoid eating disorders.

Combination of factors

The causes of eating disorders are many and complex. Most teens will probably not develop an eating disorder if they have only one of the problems mentioned. But a combination of them, as Cherry O'Neill says in her autobiography, can create "a monster":

> The individual components alone probably would not have led to such a nightmare, but together they created disaster: family instability, financial stress, my father's absences, high expectations, high visibility, perfectionism, overprotection, confused sexual identity accompanied by fear of womanhood and adult responsibilities, dread of the mere thought of sexual involvement, excessive dieting and exercise, sibling rivalry, my perceived role as mediator between family members, and unresolved grief [at the death of her grandfather, great-grandfather, and best friend]. Here was a formula for self-destruction.[56]

Like O'Neill, many teens face difficult problems. Given today's emphasis on physical perfection, it is easy for them to focus on food and appearance as a way of solving or avoiding those problems.

4

Eating Disorders in Males

MOST TEENS WITH eating disorders are girls. Knowing this, boys with eating disorders are often ashamed to admit that they have a "girls' disease." Even if they or their parents do seek help, they may be ignored or overlooked. One young man wrote to an eating disorders website that when his weight was extremely low—thirty-five pounds underweight—his parents took him to see a doctor. The doctor said, "Boys do not get anorexia. He is just losing his baby fat."[57] That doctor was wrong. Boys make up 10 percent of those with anorexia and bulimia, and they need help just as much as girls do.

The scope of the problem

The American Anorexia Bulimia Association (AABA) reports that more than five million Americans suffer from eating disorders. Others say the number is close to eight million. Even if boys and men are only 10 percent of those with anorexia and bulimia, those figures mean that between five hundred thousand and eight hundred thousand boys and men are affected. Other estimates are higher, putting the number of males potentially as high as one million. Some researchers suggest, too, that the percentage of males might be understated in statistics because boys and men are less likely to seek help for eating disorders.

Many researchers believe, too, that if statistics on binge eating were included in eating disorder statistics, the percentage of males would be greater than 10 percent. Denise Wilfley, codirector of Yale University's Center for Eating and Weight Disorders, reported in 1996 that men make up 30 percent of those in her therapy group for binge eating. Other treatment centers report an increase in the number of men seeking help for all eating disorders. However, they are not sure whether that means that more men are developing the disorders or that more men are now seeking help. "There's a need to improve our recognition of eating disorders in males and to provide more adequate treatment,"[58] says Dr. Arnold Andersen, who in addition to his medical research on eating disorders, edited and contributed to *Males with Eating Disorders.*

Male body image

Teenage boys don't face the same pressure to be thin as girls, but they do face pressures of their own—to be physically fit and muscular. *Highlights,* an online publication of the Columbia University Health Service, discusses male body image in "The Male Body: Is Rambo Our Best Choice?"

> Body image is always thought of as being a women's issue, but when one actually starts to look closely, our culture is often just as hard on men. "Acceptable" male body types in America are limited. . . . Most media images of men display the male body in the primary genre in which we celebrate it today—as an object of sporting interest. Even the NYC bus advertisements show men in their underwear with bulging muscles. This is in contrast to real living male bodies that come in all sizes and shapes, as well as degrees of physical fitness.[59]

To conform to this ideal, approximately one-quarter of boys are trying to gain weight, and boys who see themselves as thinner than average are more likely to have a negative view of their bodies. But the weight they are trying to put on is not fat, but muscle, particularly in the upper body. A trim stomach is still the cultural ideal, making the favored shape for males a V-shaped body.

The journal *Adolescence* reports on a study of body-image attitudes of high school football players (who have the large, muscular physique favored by the culture) and

While teenage boys do not face pressure to be thin, many try to increase upper body muscle mass to match the popular image of male attractiveness.

cross-country runners (who are thinner and leaner). The results showed that football players did indeed report a more positive body image, even though most of them still wanted to put on more weight. The slimmer cross-country runners, however, were less satisfied with their bodies and wanted to increase the size of their upper bodies. The article states,

> Although cross-country running requires a leaner physique, the cultural belief that males should possess a muscular body, places the runner in conflict. Also, in recent years a number of Olympic cross-country and track stars have exhibited a very lean, yet very mesomorphic [muscular] body type. This desire for a very lean, yet muscular body type is also prevalent in gymnastics which, interestingly, is a sport noted for a high incidence of eating disorders such as anorexia and bu-

limia. There is some evidence that runners may also be more prone to disordered eating behaviors, and the data from the present study indeed show that they scored higher on the bulimia and oral control portions of the EAT instrument [Eating Attitudes Test].[60]

These findings are important because dieting and exercising are two ways these athletes can change their weight or body build. And both are risk factors for eating disorders if carried to extremes.

Boys at risk

Many boys begin dieting or exercising to meet some goal of athletic achievement. Most at risk are those involved in sports where weight control is important, such as wrestlers, members of crew teams, gymnasts, lightweight football players, jockeys, and body builders. *Science News,* published on a Cornell University website, reports on a study at Cornell University and Ithaca College in upstate New York. The study found that 42 percent of lightweight football players had dysfunctional eating patterns. Of those, 74 percent had engaged in binge eating and 17 percent had made themselves vomit.

Science editor Susan Lang writes, "Athletes have been known to use such high-risk tactics as jogging in hot showers while wrapped in plastic bags, using diuretics, laxatives, steroids and amphetamines, self-inducing vomiting, fasting before weigh-ins and later gorging, and overusing saunas."[61] During one wrestling season, according to an article in *Sports Parents* magazine, three college wrestlers died in a thirty-three-day period trying to achieve their weight requirements.

Another danger to athletes is that exercise itself can be addictive. In girls, exercise addiction usually comes after a girl develops anorexia, but in boys the obsessive exercise often comes first. Tony Muno, for example, attended college on a gymnastics scholarship. He found that once he started taking off weight for competition, he couldn't stop. "I just got obsessed with it. It started to consume my thoughts."[62] When his weight reached 113 pounds—at five feet, ten inches tall—he dropped out of school and entered a hospital. He stayed there for only three months, but his entire recovery process took two and one-half years.

Too often, however, compulsive exercising gets overlooked because our culture views even extreme exercise as a virtue. A former bulimic reports that he started dieting at age fifteen in high school to stay in his division for swimming and water polo:

> I alternately starved myself (in a relative sense—I ate, but not nearly enough to sustain my activity level) and binged (donuts and halvah were favorites at the time). Thus began about 10 years of bulimia during which I exercised more and more so that I could eat as much as I wanted. No one ever knew I had a problem; people just thought that I was a good athlete. . . . I couldn't stop or I'd get "fat," a fate worse than death.[63]

Male dancers, actors, and models are also at risk for eating disorders because a slim appearance is as important to young men in these professions as it is to young women.

Homosexuality and eating disorders

Although homosexuality isn't an issue when discussing women with eating disorders, researchers and therapists report that about 21 percent of males with eating disorders are gay. Gay men tend to choose a slimmer body as their ideal than straight men, and the gay culture is more likely to equate being thin with being attractive.

In fact, gay men and men with eating disorders identify the same type of male body as ideal. A study involving male college students at a midwestern university found that "the preferred body shape for contemporary men without eating disorders was the V-shaped body, whereas the eating-disordered group strove for the 'lean, toned, thin' shape." Interestingly, when the same researchers asked about the ideal female body shape, both groups responded most with "thin, slim, slightly underweight."[64]

Awareness that a number of men with eating disorders are gay makes some teens and men reluctant to seek help. Heterosexuals are afraid of being considered gay, and some who are gay do not want to reveal their sexual orien-

A cross-country runner's physique, usually thin and lean, may be at odds with cultural ideas about male attractiveness.

tation in the course of treatment. Still, most men with eating disorders are straight. Having an eating disorder does not indicate that a teenager is gay.

Similarities with girls

Teenagers with eating disorders have many things in common, whether they are boys or girls. Like girls, teenage boys are living in a society in which gender roles are changing, and they, too, can be confused about what is expected of them. In addition to a similar preoccupation with body image, both boys and girls can have low self-esteem and suffer from depression. Young men as well as women can come from dysfunctional families where drugs or alcohol are abused. Some were abused themselves as children. Others use food as a comfort when sad or anxious.

Jonathan, a young man who was treated for depression and bulimia, says, "My parents expressed their love through food. My mother colluded [cooperated] with my overeating—I'd eat an entire tub of ice cream, and she wouldn't ask where it had gone."[65] He weighed 392 pounds when he finally went for counseling at age seventeen. There he confronted many issues—his homosexuality, a strained relationship with his parents, and fear of rejection.

Teenage boys with eating disorders can also be perfectionists and obsessive. Many often feel unworthy and don't like themselves. One man who suffered from bulimia for years remembers the low self-esteem he felt as a teen when he turned to food for comfort. Other teenage boys start to diet in response to teasing from friends. Then, when they are praised for losing weight, they keep on losing. Like girls, "they believe that losing weight will help them to be accepted and it will make them happy."[66]

Control is another issue. Researchers have found that, like women, men with eating disorders often don't feel in control of their lives. They may come from families where their independence isn't encouraged or respected. Changing their bodies can give them a feeling of power and control.

Young men can also suffer from chemical imbalances that cause depression and obsessive behavior. In addition, it is known that men with anorexia have a lower level of the male hormone testosterone.

Differences with girls

There are, however, some important differences between young men and women with eating disorders. One is the average age of onset. In teenage girls, anorexia shows itself as early as thirteen or fourteen, while in males it appears in the late teens or early twenties. Other differences involve actual body weight at the onset of the disorder. Girls who develop eating disorders say they feel fat when they begin dieting, but they are usually at or close to normal weight. Most boys, on the other hand, are in fact overweight when they begin their regimen of dieting and exercise. Researcher and writer Arnold Andersen says that "more men who develop anorexia or bulimia were seriously teased as overweight children."[67]

Another difference is that, while girls diet to become thin, boys are more concerned with body shape and muscle definition. They often begin dieting and exercising to meet the criteria of a particular sport. Perhaps this is why they are more likely to use excessive exercise as a way of getting rid of calories, rather than taking laxatives or vomiting.

Some young men also begin dieting as a way to avoid weight-related illnesses that they see in their fathers and other family members. For example, if they are overweight and see their obese fathers with heart problems, they may be determined to lose weight and live a healthier lifestyle. Then, as with young women, when other psychological problems are present, the dieting becomes uncontrollable.

More research needed

Because girls and women make up the vast majority of those with eating disorders, most research has centered on them. But more research is needed on boys and men. Yale University's Denise Wilfley says this about her study of compulsive eaters:

> In some cases dieting has been shown to trigger binge eating, but more research is needed to uncover other triggers, particularly in men. For example, many of the men in our treatment program were overweight as children and began binge eating at an early age. That could mean the problem is genetically based or [that something in the family climate sets up situations in which] children turn to food to cope with stress.[68]

Other men in her study were school athletes in their teen years and developed a pattern of eating large quantities of food. This led to weight problems when they were no longer physically active. However, she adds, "because studies of men with binge eating disorders are so few, researchers still have a lot to learn."[69]

One thing researchers do know is that the consequences of eating disorders cross gender lines. The medical complications caused by starvation, bingeing and purging are similar for both males and females.

5

Dangers of Eating Disorders

ANYONE CAN LOOK at a person starving from anorexia and know that something is wrong. But the anoretic's thin, skeletal look tells only a small part of what is happening inside that person's body. The consequences of bulimia are even more hidden because a person with bulimia is usually close to a normal weight. Even a compulsive eater is not necessarily grossly obese. But in all cases, the eating disorder has serious effects on the body. Some can be permanent and even life threatening.

Physical dangers of anorexia

People with anorexia are literally starving themselves, and their bodies show signs of starvation. Some signs are easily noticed. These include a lack of energy, feeling cold all the time, inability to sleep, dry patchy hair from a loss of protein, dizziness, headaches, constipation from lack of food and fluids, and the growth of lanugo, fine hair that grows all over the body as a way to conserve heat.

Other signs are not as obvious, but more dangerous. Anoretics can develop low blood pressure, an irregular heartbeat, and eventually heart failure. Kathy, whose story appears in Chapter 1, died of heart failure, as did singing star Karen Carpenter, who fought an eight-year battle with anorexia. And fifteen-year-old Alicia Mitchell, who was featured on a *48 Hours* documentary about weight and dieting, had already suffered a heart attack.

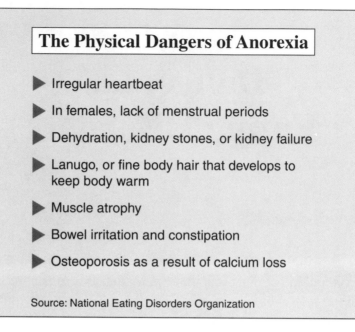

The Physical Dangers of Anorexia

▶ Irregular heartbeat

▶ In females, lack of menstrual periods

▶ Dehydration, kidney stones, or kidney failure

▶ Lanugo, or fine body hair that develops to keep body warm

▶ Muscle atrophy

▶ Bowel irritation and constipation

▶ Osteoporosis as a result of calcium loss

Source: National Eating Disorders Organization

Alicia also had kidney problems, another consequence of anorexia. Not only does the starving body become dehydrated, but people with eating disorders often aggravate their fluid loss by taking diuretics. Kidney function is affected because a dehydrated body has low levels of electrolytes, such as potassium, which are necessary for the kidneys to work properly.

Potassium deficiency can also cause problems with muscle contractions, including the heart muscle. In fact, the National Association of Anorexia Nervosa and Associated Disorders (ANAD) states that the most common cause of death in a long-time anoretic is low serum potassium, which can cause an irregular heartbeat.

Reproductive changes

As the body loses fat, the reproductive system gradually shuts down. Girls stop menstruating when their estrogen levels drop, a condition called amenorrhea. Or, if the girl is very young, the onset of menstruation will be delayed. Although fifteen, Alicia Mitchell still has the body of a child. Her mother states that Alicia stopped growing physically at the age of nine.

The loss of estrogen in teenage girls can cause another problem—loss of bone mass, which leads to osteoporosis. Osteoporosis is a disease in which bones lose their density and become weak and brittle. It is most common in older women who have gone through menopause, but if a teen is no longer producing estrogen, she, too, is at risk. Loss of bone mass means that the bones can break easily. Weak, brittle bones can also lead to abnormal curvature of the spine.

Physical dangers of bulimia

Many anoretics are also bulimic—and even bulimics who are not anorexic often have periods of fasting as well as bingeing. As a result, bulimics share many symptoms with anoretics. These can include lack of energy, loss of menstruation, dehydration, constipation, and electrolyte and other nutritional imbalances, which can lead to heart and kidney problems. In addition, repeated vomiting puts a great strain on the body.

Stomach acid in the vomit, for example, can cause sore throats and tooth decay. Cherry O'Neill reports that although she was fortunate to recover from most of her physical problems, she had to have all of her teeth capped because they were so badly damaged. Even more serious is damage to the esophagus, the tube that leads from the mouth to the stomach. The esophagus can develop sores from stomach acid and, in severe cases, can even rupture and cause death. Repeated vomiting also causes infected salivary glands, which make the face look swollen.

Dangerous ways to lose weight

Many anoretics and bulimics misuse drugs and medications to help them lose weight. The website *Mirror-Mirror: Eating Disorders Shared Awareness* discusses syrup of ipecac, laxatives, diuretics, and diet pills. All of these can be dangerous if taken in large quantities or for longer periods than recommended.

Syrup of ipecac is used to induce vomiting. Most families with small children have a bottle on hand in case of accidental poisoning. It should never be used for any other reason, however, as it is a powerful drug. It stays in the body's cells for a time and repeated use can cause chest pains and heart problems, including irregular heartbeat, rapid heart rate, or cardiac arrest.

More common is the use of laxatives. Bulimics think they are losing weight when taking laxatives, but in fact, these drugs have little or no effect on weight loss. By the time laxatives work, the calories have already been absorbed. People feel they have lost weight because fluid was lost, but the body will start to retain water again. Then they will feel bloated and take laxatives again.

Abuse of laxatives can harm the body, causing "bloody diarrhea, electrolyte imbalances and dehydration. Many people find that after prolonged use they cannot move their bowels without them. . . . Laxative abuse . . . can lead to permanent damage to the bowels, severe medical compli-

cations and even death."[70] Cherry O'Neill writes that she once took sixty laxative tablets, resulting in uncontrollable diarrhea, as well as severe cramping and pain.

Diuretics, or water pills, cause the body to lose fluids through urination. But as with laxatives, this is a temporary loss. In the meantime, though, repeated use of diuretics can lead to dehydration and subsequent kidney damage. Overusing diuretics can also cause electrolyte imbalances, which can affect vital organs such as the heart, kidneys, and liver, and put a person at high risk for heart failure.

Diet pills, too, can be harmful, even though many types can be bought over the counter without a prescription. They contain stimulants that can cause increased heart rate, dizziness, high blood pressure, nausea, anxiety, irritability, insomnia, dry mouth, and diarrhea. For any person who is truly overweight, but otherwise in good health, the safest way to lose pounds is to eat balanced, nutritious meals and exercise moderately.

Physical dangers of compulsive eating

Compulsive eating is not as life threatening as anorexia and bulimia, but it is dangerous when it leads to obesity. People are said to be obese when they are 25 percent above normal weight or have a BMI of 30 or more. Obesity can lead to high blood pressure, high cholesterol levels, and other conditions that can lead to heart problems. In addition, bingeing on sweet foods can make the pancreas work overtime to produce insulin, which puts a person at risk of developing diabetes.

Psychological consequences of eating disorders

Eating disorders also have psychological consequences. Studies have shown that victims of severe famine experience chemical changes in their nervous systems. These abnormalities cause personality changes, and the victims tend to become depressed, anxious, irritable, and irrational, with wide swings in mood. Many also become preoccupied with food and develop strange tastes for foods. The same characteristics are typical of anoretics.

LeAdelle Phelps and Ellen Bajorek discuss these and other behaviors in *School Psychology Review:*

> The person with anorexia often thinks in dichotomous [either/or] terms, for example that he/she is in complete control or completely out of control. Thus starvation represents an assertion of control, and control is important because the body and the mind are not to be trusted. . . . As the person with anorexia becomes socially withdrawn and loses interest in activities previously thought to be important, schoolwork, intensive exercising, and dieting become the entire focus of her/his life. Because the caloric intake is insufficient for the high activity level, work productivity and concentration decrease. . . . This "starved" individual displays impaired concentration and alertness.[71]

Bulimics also experience anxiety and depression, although, as noted before, depression often exists before the disease and is a factor in developing bulimia. However, the shame and guilt bulimics feel at their bingeing can add to their depression.

In addition, bulimics can get caught up in a vicious cycle, as Suzanne Abraham and Derek Llewellyn-Jones explain in their book, *Eating Disorders: The Facts.* Bulimics use the binge as a way to relieve stress and anxiety, and actually do feel freer while they are bingeing. They also experience a sense of release when purging. However, they then may feel guilt at the vomiting and worry that they will gain weight from the binge. The result is increased anxiety, depression, and low self-esteem, leading to more bingeing.

Compulsive eaters do not experience changes in brain chemistry like the anoretic, but they do feel the shame that the bulimic feels when bingeing. In addition, they suffer from low self-esteem and a poor body image. Obesity can be especially hard on children, who are teased by their classmates, and on teens, who are not only teased, but have trouble getting dates as well.

Loss of control

Many people with eating disorders think they are controlling their lives, but the disease ends up controlling them. Cherry O'Neill spent years fighting her disorder and suffered many relapses. She writes:

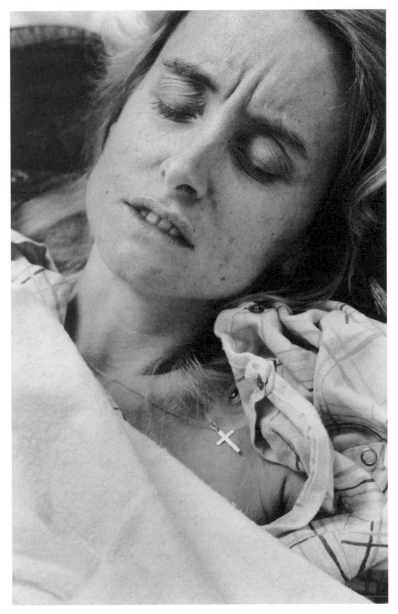

Eating disorders can cause depression, irritability, irrational behavior, and mood swings. These problems are caused by chemical changes in the nervous system brought on by starving oneself.

I began sincere efforts to change my behavior: eating without vomiting, forgoing an occasional hour of exercise, having a substantial meal without allowing it to trigger a binge. In spite of my attempts, however, the other part of me (apparently the more influential part) always succeeded in undermining my good intentions. My neurosis had become too deep and too obsessive to be easily dismissed. . . . Incredibly,

the area of my life in which I had prided myself for having to-
tal control had now taken control of me, so much so that I was
feeling trapped and helpless.[72]

Getting help

None of the problems caused by eating disorders happen overnight. Some can take years to develop. The longer
an eating disorder persists, however, the harder it is to
overcome—and the more damage is done to the body. The
best way for teens to avoid the life-threatening consequences of an eating disorder is to ask for help as soon as a
problem with food is suspected.

6

Treatment of Eating Disorders

THERE ARE MANY places where teenagers can receive treatment for an eating disorder. Parents, counselors, and physicians can help them find a program that meets their needs. Most programs are outpatient, where the teen lives at home but goes to the treatment center daily or a few times a week. Eating disorder specialist Dr. Joanne Witkowski believes outpatient treatment is more effective than inpatient because it enables people to work out family relationships and problems as they deal with their eating disorder.

However, sometimes an inpatient center is necessary. Outpatient treatment may have failed, the teen may be in danger of dying from medical complications, or the family situation might be unstable and even contributing to the problem. Different centers have different philosophies of care and costs vary, so it is important for families to learn about a center and talk to the therapists.

In the past, treatment often included forced feeding, tube feeding, or drugs to stimulate appetite. Today, however, therapists realize that these techniques result in only temporary weight gains, and patients return to the disordered eating as soon as they are released. Although intravenous feeding is still used for patients who are very ill, good treatment centers look for the underlying causes of the eating disorder. Then they can help patients learn or relearn normal eating habits.

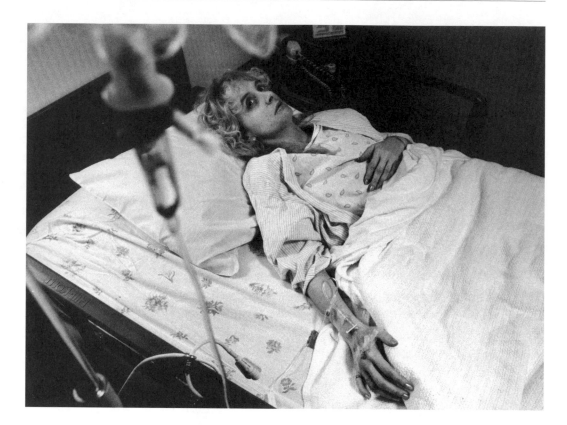

An anoretic is hospitalized and treated for her disease. Although intravenous feeding is still used on very ill patients, good treatment centers concentrate on the underlying causes of the eating disorder.

Making a diagnosis

When an eating disorder is suspected, the best place to start looking for help is the teen's pediatrician or family physician. Many doctors begin with a series of questions, developed by mental health professionals, to explore attitudes and behavior regarding food. They include questions such as: What is your weight right now? Do you think you're too fat or that parts of your body are too fat? Over the past few months, has your weight increased, decreased, or remained the same? Anoretics and bulimics have an unrealistic view of their weight. Anoretics also single out parts of their bodies, like their stomach or thighs, as being too fat.

The doctor will also ask about dieting and other means of losing weight, such as using laxatives or diuretics. How much a teen exercises, too, is important. Boys, especially, use excessive exercise as a way to burn calories.

Attitudes toward eating and weight gain are explored with questions such as: Have you ever felt your eating is out of control? What would you consider your perfect weight? How would a weight increase or decrease of five pounds affect you?

The doctor further explores the patient's eating habits. Unusual eating habits, such as eating alone, insisting on a certain plate, always eating food in a particular order, or eating only certain kinds of food, may all be signs of an eating disorder. And in girls, the absence of menstruation is another sign.

Sometimes even getting someone to the doctor can be difficult, as most people with anorexia deny that anything is wrong. Cherry O'Neill, for example, was seventeen years old and down to ninety-two pounds, seriously underweight at five feet, seven inches tall. Yet, when her parents discovered how thin she was, her reaction was anger and denial that she had a problem:

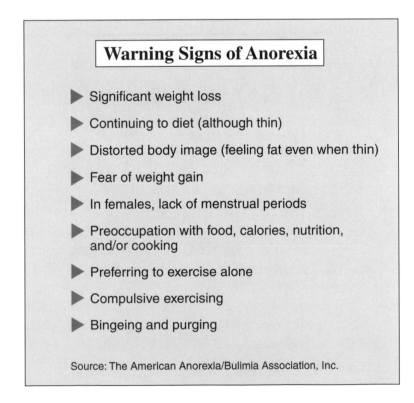

Warning Signs of Anorexia

▶ Significant weight loss

▶ Continuing to diet (although thin)

▶ Distorted body image (feeling fat even when thin)

▶ Fear of weight gain

▶ In females, lack of menstrual periods

▶ Preoccupation with food, calories, nutrition, and/or cooking

▶ Preferring to exercise alone

▶ Compulsive exercising

▶ Bingeing and purging

Source: The American Anorexia/Bulimia Association, Inc.

"Cherry, honey, you're nothing but skin and bones! We've got to take you in to see the doctor tomorrow and find out what the problem is." My dad's voice continued as did my mother's tears, but my attentiveness came to a screeching halt as panic curbed my willingness to listen.

"I'm not sick!" I objected. "I feel fine! I don't need to see a doctor!"

"Cherry," my mother moaned, "I just saw your back and you look like a concentration-camp victim. You may feel all right but you look like a skeleton!"

My anger was mounting as I realized that not only were they threatening to jeopardize the area of my life that had become most important to me, but they had invaded my privacy!

[Cherry continued to fight with her parents about seeing a doctor.] "It's *my* body!" I argued. "I know how I feel, and I'm not sick! I'm not hurting anyone else by being thin, so why should it bother you? I'll tell you if I need a doctor."[73]

Cherry's denial of a problem doomed early treatment attempts to failure. Her obsession with dieting and food had

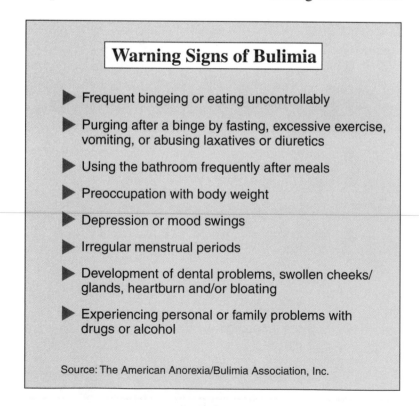

Warning Signs of Bulimia

▶ Frequent bingeing or eating uncontrollably

▶ Purging after a binge by fasting, excessive exercise, vomiting, or abusing laxatives or diuretics

▶ Using the bathroom frequently after meals

▶ Preoccupation with body weight

▶ Depression or mood swings

▶ Irregular menstrual periods

▶ Development of dental problems, swollen cheeks/glands, heartburn and/or bloating

▶ Experiencing personal or family problems with drugs or alcohol

Source: The American Anorexia/Bulimia Association, Inc.

become a control issue between herself and her parents. Cherry's thinking had to change before her behavior could.

Team approach

Experts agree that a team approach is the best way to change thinking and behavior. The team consists of the family physician to monitor physical health, a nutritionist to teach the patient normal eating habits, and a psychotherapist to explore reasons behind the eating disorder and to help the patient overcome her destructive eating patterns.

The team will start with a thorough medical exam, checking blood chemistry, blood pressure, and heart rate. They will also look for swollen salivary glands, damaged teeth enamel, and calluses on the hands from rubbing on the teeth when inducing vomiting. The nutritionist will take a diet history and try to learn the patient's calorie intake. A psychiatric evaluation will explore moods, sleeping patterns, thoughts of suicide, and childhood and family background, to see if there is a history of depression, substance abuse, and other problems.

Types of therapy

Treatment involves a combination of approaches using both individual and group therapy. In group therapy, a therapist helps guide the discussion among people with the same problem. A group can help to get to the heart of a person's problem. Teenagers with anorexia and bulimia can talk freely to other teens concerning their feelings about food and how they are trying to get well. Being in a group of people with the same problems also makes it harder for individuals to say, as they might to a therapist, "You just don't understand."

Dr. David Rube, director of psychiatry at The Children's Medical Center in Dayton, Ohio, told *Family Life* reporter Debbie Allen that "a support group is essential because anorexia is a disorder of withdrawal. As anorexia sufferers become more obsessed with food and exercise, they withdraw from family, friends and other social contacts."[74] A group program gets them talking with others again.

However, group therapy alone is not enough. Individual therapy with a counselor is needed to help people learn what is really happening with their eating disorder. Anoretics like Cherry O'Neill, for example, see not-eating as a form of control. They panic, thinking that if they fail to control their eating, they will lose control over other aspects of their lives as well. Others use the eating disorder as a focus to prevent thinking about other problems. The family, too, may use the teen's anorexia as a way to avoid facing family problems. Bulimics and compulsive eaters eat for comfort or as a way to ease anxiety. Psychotherapy helps them to understand what triggers their binges and to find other ways of handling their feelings. It also helps them develop a sense of self-worth that is not dependent on their weight.

Other aspects of treatment work directly to change the eating behavior. Behavioral therapy is one method. With this treatment, writes eating disorders specialist Suzanne Abraham,

> the therapist attempts to induce the patient to modify or to change her behavior, by providing rewards or privileges, so that she learns to eat normally. For example, if a patient who has anorexia nervosa gains weight, or if a patient with bulimia reduces the frequency of self-induced vomiting, or if the obese person loses weight, a reward is given.[75]

Cognitive-behavioral therapy

According to Abraham, however, the most effective individual treatment is cognitive-behavioral therapy. The word cognitive refers to mental processes and what we know or believe. Cognitive-behavioral therapy, then, tries to change a person's way of thinking. "People with eating disorders have distorted thinking," says Dr. Witkowski of Kaiser-Permanente. "Negative thoughts have to become positive. They have to learn when they're looking at things incorrectly."[76]

The therapist works with the patient to change her distorted thinking about weight and food. One way is to keep a thought journal, in which she writes down things she be-

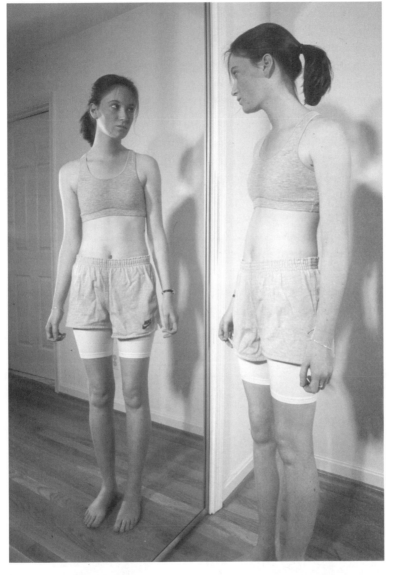

Cognitive-behavioral therapy tries to teach the anoretic or bulimic a new way of thinking about feelings, needs, and self-image.

lieves. For example, she might write, "If I gain weight, no one will want to hang out with me." Then she and the therapist can discuss whether this is really true.

Peggy Claude-Pierre's therapy of unconditional love is also a form of cognitive-behavioral therapy. In her treatment, the therapist has to "recognize the negative mindset and create an alliance with the victim against it."[77] Patients keep journals of their feelings. They use two columns. In one they write their negative thoughts, in the other a rational comeback. As they recover, the rational side becomes stronger.

Cognitive-behavioral therapy is especially effective with bulimics. Abraham urges her patients to keep a mood diary and a food diary. The food diary records everything the patient eats, what time she eats, and how much. The mood diary tells what thoughts and feelings she has during eating. The purpose is to help the person to see the relationship between how she feels and what she eats. Eventually the therapist helps the patient to develop more healthy ways of dealing with her feelings.

Cognitive-behavioral therapy is more difficult with anoretics because their thoughts about body weight and shape are so rigid. Their self-esteem is bound in their weight and shape and they think about these two things all day. "Their rigidity of thought makes change harder to achieve,"[78] says Abraham.

Medication

Many experts believe that chemical imbalances in the brain are a cause of eating disorders. This is supported by evidence that eating disorders can run in families and that many bulimics suffer from depression. In the 1980s, researchers learned that antidepressant medication can lessen the number of binges, at least in the short term. In fact, the American Anorexia Bulimia Association (AABA) reports that 50–90 percent of bulimics binge less often when they are on antidepressants.

Antidepressants also lessen depression and feelings of hopelessness. They make a person feel happier and more energetic. But they are not "magic pills." They don't cure bulimia. They work by making the urge to binge less powerful. Some antidepressant drugs, like Prozac, can also lessen the compulsion to exercise and the obsession with food and weight. The best treatment for bulimia today involves a combination of medication and cognitive-behavioral therapy.

Compulsive eaters are helped by antidepressants, too, although they also benefit from psychotherapy and behavioral therapy. Anoretics present a different story. The AABA reports that only Prozac has been shown to help in the treatment of anorexia. And according to Abraham and Llewellyn-Jones, antidepressants help only a small number of anoretics. Unlike bulimics, they are no more likely to be depressed than women without an eating disorder. In most cases, depression felt by anoretics disappears when they gain weight and recover.

Obstacles to recovery

Eating disorders, especially anorexia, are difficult to treat because the disease becomes part of the person's identity. Cindy Lauer said on CNN's IMPACT, "The eating disorder has sort of evolved into who I am. I already feel bad enough about myself, but . . . even though it's unhealthy, I have some way of defining myself. And I am just afraid that once I get better, I am just going to be an empty

'For heaven's sake Jackie, forget the diet for one day.'

shell."[79] One adult bulimic wondered how she was going to fill her days if she wasn't planning her binges and purges all the time.

In addition, the eating disorder may actually have some perceived benefits. As the eating disorder takes over more of a girl's life, she can reduce the pressures on herself and avoid making decisions. Abraham reports that patients have said, "If I am thin, people know there is something wrong and do not expect as much."[80] The illness can also be a way for the family to avoid seeing other problems because they focus all their attention on the daughter or son with the eating disorder.

Compulsive eating leading to obesity can also release the eater from pressures that had threatened to overwhelm her. One teen dropped out of competitive swimming at age twelve and began to put on weight until, at age nineteen, she weighed 238 pounds. She wrote, "All the girls were too competitive. I'm out of that now, and can get on with everyone. When I was swimming people picked on me if I didn't do as well as they expected me to have done. Now I can do what I like, and do the things I like well."[81]

Helping a friend

Teenagers can help friends with eating disorders. For example, if teens go out in a group and see that a friend has stopped eating—or eats large amounts of food and goes to the bathroom to throw up—they can talk to the problem eater. The best approach is to find a private moment when they can say that they are worried about the person, rather than criticizing his or her behavior. They can also suggest that the person talk to a doctor or a counselor. If the friend reacts with anger or denies that the behavior in question is abnormal, it is fruitless to prolong the discussion or to argue. The matter may be brought up again, but it is important to understand that denial is part of the illness.

Teenagers themselves cannot cure anyone or make anyone go for treatment, and indeed they may mistake a passing bad mood or an actual case of illness for symptoms of an eating disorder. However, if a friend seems suicidal or dangerously ill, a caring adult should be told—a parent, teacher, or school counselor.

Treatment for eating disorders is a long process, and relapses are common. Even after treatment, a person should have access to his or her therapist. Not everyone succeeds in banishing these dangerous conditions, but experts agree that the earlier treatment begins, the greater the chance of a full recovery.

7

Prevention of
Eating Disorders

THE BEST TREATMENT for eating disorders, as with any illness, is prevention. Teenagers who feel good about themselves and who have a positive and healthy attitude toward their bodies are less likely to develop eating disorders. Some schools now have programs in which young people learn to value themselves. Eating disorder organizations, too, offer educational programs to increase awareness of society's obsession with being thin.

Looking at weight realistically

One way teens can help themselves is to look at their weight realistically and to understand that superslim models and actors are underweight. The female body is supposed to have some fat in preparation for childbearing. "If society were in concert with how females actually develop, we'd celebrate the rounding of the female shape around puberty," says Yale University professor of psychology Kelly D. Brownell. "But because women are told to be thin, adolescence signals the onset of a fight with the body that never ends."[82]

It doesn't have to be that way, though. Teenagers today can learn the facts about diet and weight, and they can stop destructive habits before they become firmly entrenched. Most of all, teens who fall within acceptable weight guidelines can decide not to diet. They can decide not to put themselves at risk for eating disorders. They can remember that most diets don't work at all, or only work in the short term. About 95 percent of all dieters regain their lost pounds within a few years—and many will gain more weight than they originally lost.

In addition, people who are average weight when they diet, as many teenage girls are, do not lose any weight at all over a six-month period. All the counting calories, stepping on scales, and depriving themselves of food they enjoy yield no results.

Some scientists believe that this is because each person's body has a "set point," the weight at which it operates most efficiently. The body tries to maintain this weight. If a person diets and begins losing weight, the body reacts by slowing its metabolism to prevent further weight loss. Then, if the person starts eating normally again, he or she might actually gain more weight. That is why most physicians recommend both diet and exercise

Teenagers who feel good about themselves are more likely to resist pressure to imitate superslim models and actresses and less likely to develop eating disorders.

for people who really need to lose weight. Exercise—when done in moderation—is fun and healthy, and it helps a person lose weight by burning calories and increasing metabolism.

Positive thinking

Not everyone can look like a supermodel or a superathlete, and unsupervised attempts to achieve such effects can result in serious bodily harm. People come in all sizes and shapes. Being thin does not mean being happy. To learn to enjoy their bodies as they are, teenagers can find a sport that suits their body—soccer, basketball, skating, skiing, baseball, tennis, swimming—and enjoy it. Girls especially can start to value their bodies for what they can do, not for how they look to others.

Girls must value their bodies for what they can do, not for how they look to others.

Just as important, teens can help their friends by not teasing them about their weight. When someone who is not overweight at all, or only slightly, says, "I'm so fat," friends can say, "No you're not. Your weight is okay." Peer pressure, which pushes some teens to start dieting, can work the other way, too. In addition, teenagers can do more than discourage friends from starting a needless or very strict diet—they can also talk to friends they think might be having a problem with food. Early talks might help a friend realize something is wrong.

Teens can also try to understand their emotions. Sadness, anger, or boredom should not be confused with hunger. If teenagers talk to their parents about family problems and issues of control, they will be less tempted to rely on food as a means of exerting some control. Perhaps most important is love and acceptance of oneself. This can be a hard goal to achieve. The organization Eating Disorders Awareness and Prevention (EDAP) makes the following suggestions:

> Next time a "thin" thought attacks, try changing your mental tape to one of these messages:
>
> When you look in the mirror, catch yourself before you say something negative. Say something positive. It'll feel better.
>
> Keep a Top-10 list of things you already like about yourself. Add to your list often.
>
> Eat when you are hungry. Rest when you are tired. Surround yourself with people and possessions that remind you of your inner strength and beauty.[83]

Help in schools

Not everyone can go it alone, but fortunately, some schools are stepping in to help. The *News-Journal* in Daytona Beach, Florida, reports on some local schools in north central Florida that recognize the importance of self-esteem and offer programs to help young teens gain confidence and feel good about themselves. One middle school in Bunnell, for example, devotes the first period each day to a Prime Time class. Activities are built around goal setting, responsibility, building relationships, and self-control.

Another school, Port Orange's Atlantic High School, offers students a six-week course to help build self-confidence. "Teachers refer students who they feel have self-esteem issues," says guidance director Allene Dupont. "The students need to realize they can shape their lives by the choices they make and that they do have control—although not about everything in life—and can help direct their lives." [84] Feeling in control of their lives can help teens resist seeing food and weight as the only things they can control.

Eating Disorders Awareness Week

Many groups today are working to prevent and treat eating disorders. There is even an annual Eating Disorders Awareness Week, sponsored by EDAP. Held in February, the week features local activities across the country coordinated by a network of volunteers. The purpose of the week is to "enhance public awareness of eating disorders and to challenge cultural attitudes and values contributing to eating disorders." [85] Posters, buttons and T-shirts carry the theme: Don't Weigh Your Self-Esteem. . . . It's What's Inside that Counts.

Targeted audiences are high school and college students, families, parents, school personnel, and professionals who work with young people. Some Eating Disorders Awareness Weeks have concentrated on high-risk groups, such as athletes, compulsive exercisers, and models, and on those who influence those groups—coaches, school personnel, and the sports, entertainment, and advertising industries.

Media campaign

EDAP's Media Advocacy Campaign, which started in the fall of 1997, is open to participation by teenagers. With help from people all over the country, EDAP looks for advertisements that "glorify thinness at the expense of physical and emotional health, as well as those that promote healthy self-esteem and body image." [86] Every month they choose at least one ad that sends "healthy body image signals" and one that sends "potentially negative body image messages," and they write a letter to the companies' advertising departments.

There are many reasons to exercise—health and fitness, stress reduction, and pure enjoyment.

For example, in March 1998, EDAP wrote a letter to Avia shoes, whose ad showed a very thin model in exercise clothes jumping rope. The text read: "She trained for many reasons, including rocky road ice cream. Our shoes are a stable and comfortable platform for your highest aspirations." EDAP wrote:

We agree that there are many reasons for exercise: for overall health and fitness, stress reduction, entertainment, feelings of strength and accomplishment, and for pure enjoyment. Unfortunately, the woman in your advertisement sends the message that purging the body of regretted calories should be the primary reason for exercise. We couldn't disagree more. . . .

Your advertisement sends the message that some foods, like rocky road ice cream, are sinful and need to be purged from the body, in this case through exercise, and that women need to exercise in order to deserve these foods. This advertisement perpetuates a climate in which women's obsession with weight-loss is not only acceptable and expected, but completely normal and even admirable.[87]

A month later, Avia's advertising director called EDAP to say that the ad would be discontinued and that future ads would try to "promote healthy body image and self-esteem in all people, regardless of their shape or size."[88]

EDAP also wrote to the fashion magazine *Elle,* protesting two fashion layouts that featured ultrathin models:

We are writing to voice our concern and disappointment in regard to your magazine's June 1998 fashion layouts. Both "A Touch of Dusk" and "Modern Jazz" glamorize emaciated models and contribute to a cultural context that leads women to believe that celebrations of fashion and beauty are reserved only for the slender.[89]

Changes in advertising

On the positive side, EDAP wrote a letter of appreciation to Nike for its ad celebrating the skill and passion of basketball player Dawn Staley. The copy refers to her as "a giant" and says she is "eight feet tall," even though she is really five feet, six inches tall:

When what matters is the size of your passion, everything about her is outsized: her heart, her creativity, her appetite for the game. And she grows with every no-look pass, every surge past a defender . . . Air Flight Deny. [Shoes] designed for speed, creativity, extreme energy. Designed to let Dawn Staley be huge.[90]

Also praised was Champion sportswear for its ad featuring three real women walking on the beach. The copy said: "Because every woman has the right to be a Champion."[91] The Kellogg company received a letter, too, for its new Special K advertising campaign, "Reshape Your Attitude."

Teens can become involved in this program by looking at ads critically themselves. Either positive or negative examples can be reported to EDAP by clicking on "I Want to Submit an Ad" at the organization's Media Advocacy website (http://members.aol.com/edapwatch/aboutmedia.html).

New ways of thinking

There are other signs that people are becoming less accepting of the thinness ideal. In 1996, the British marketing manager for the Omega Watch Company said the company would stop advertising in the British edition of *Vogue* magazine. He said that its use of ultrathin models could encourage young women to develop eating disorders. He was referring to two features in the June issue which showed models Trish Goff and Annie Morton looking especially gaunt. Omega changed its mind about withdrawing its advertising from the magazine, but the incident was widely reported and focused attention on eating disorders in relation to the look promoted by high fashion magazines.

On a more positive note, *Titanic* star Kate Winslet shows no signs of starving herself to please others. She has been quoted as saying, "People think that if a woman isn't rail-thin, there must be something wrong with her. It's such nonsense. This is me, like it or lump it,"[92] and "I've been to hell and back with my weight, and I'm finally happy the way I am. I feel it's my responsibility as an actress to say to young women who are in turmoil about their weight that life is short, and it's here to be lived!"[93]

Even more encouraging, some women are making it as models even though they're not thin. Christine Alt says in her *Glamour* article that she is happy and successful as a size-twelve model. And the same *48 Hours* show that reported on anorexia victim Alicia Mitchell also reported on twenty-eight-year-old Jody Miller, who recently signed a contract with Plus Models in New York.

Jody is five feet, nine inches tall and weighs 165 pounds. She spent years fighting her weight. "I'd lose and I'd gain. I'd lose and I'd gain. . . . I would do anything not to eat, anything to have a flatter stomach, to look better, wear smaller—smaller clothes. . . . In high school we'd see who could go the longest without eating and I think my longest was four or five days."[94]

Actress Kate Winslet has urged young women to think realistically about their bodies and their lives.

Eventually she became bulimic, throwing up four to five times a day. It wasn't until she married that she was able to start accepting herself for who she was. Her husband helped, for he loved her the way she was. "She is very curvaceous," he told CBS. "She's all woman."[95]

As a Plus Model, Jody won't be doing high fashion. But the agency thinks she'll be perfect as a model for many nationally known stores such as J. C. Penney. More important, Jody Miller can say, "I think I'm beautiful. . . . I'm 5'9", I can stand tall and I can be OK with that. I can wear a size 14 and it's OK."[96]

More encouraging signs

Mode, a magazine for large women, launched the magazine's first Mode Awards in March 1998. The awards honor women who have improved the perception of larger women. Honors were given to actress Delta Burke, talk show host Rosie O'Donnell, U.S. secretary of state Madeleine Albright, and Judith Jamison, artistic director of the Alvin Ailey dance company. In addition, *Newsweek* reported in August 1998 that *Mode* will launch a new magazine called *Girls,* for girls of all shapes and sizes.

Others, too, are realizing that thin isn't the only way to be. In 1994, *People* magazine selected size-fourteen model Emme as one of its 50 Most Beautiful People—and fashion designers are putting together collections for larger sizes. Lane Bryant, a store with fashions for larger women, is going to have a new line for teens and those in their twenties. Even some Barbies, although still thin, are getting a more natural looking figure. In 1998, Mattel brought out a new Barbie, one with a wider waist, slimmer hips, and a smaller bust. The company is also looking ahead. "Who knows?" said Barbie division head Jean McKenzie in a *Wall Street Journal* article. "Maybe in the future Barbie will have a friend who's a little heavyset."[97]

Most encouraging are the opinions of young teens and preteens today. Readers of *Girls' Life,* a magazine for preteens, responded to a questionnaire about body image from the magazine's editors:

Many girls (83 percent) say they would never not like someone because of her body type. Almost the same number (74 percent) report that they would never make fun of a friend (or anyone else, for that matter) for being overweight. Most girls say their friends actually are simply big-boned, super-athletic or just happen to come from a family with a history of larger builds. And anyone who would make fun of someone for those reasons is, to quote one reader, "stupid."[98]

Living a healthy life

Human bodies come in all shapes and sizes. As EDAP says, people should appreciate themselves for all that they are—"everyone should respect themselves, enjoy playing and being active, and eat a variety of healthy foods."[99]

Jean Rubel, the founder of a national eating disorder organization, battled anorexia and bulimia for twelve years. She writes:

> In retrospect, being thin was such a dead end. Sometimes I think about growing old and sitting in a rocking chair with children at my feet. They will say, "Jean, tell us stories. What did you do with your life?" How pathetic if the only thing I'd ever accomplished was being thin.

> What I'm planning to say instead is that I lived well, loved a lot of people, and laughed often with my friends. I wrote books, published a newsletter, built a hospital program, and ran a national organization for several decades. I will tell them that I conquered both anorexia and bulimia and lived to a ripe old age with style and pizzazz.[100]

Teens have their whole lives to accomplish great things. They can, too, if they believe in themselves and develop eating habits that keep them healthy and strong.

Notes

Introduction

1. Dan Rather, "Fight for Life," *48 Hours,* CBS News, February 26, 1998.
2. Rhoda Unger and Mary Crawford, *Women and Gender: A Feminist Psychology.* New York: McGraw Hill, 1992, p. 588.
3. Kelli McNeill, "Starving for Attention," *American Fitness,* July/August 1995, p. 36+. (www.ebscohost.com)

Chapter 1: What Is an Eating Disorder?

4. Kathy's mother, interview by author, July 20, 1998.
5. Judith Anderson, "Battling Bulimia: My War Story," *Glamour,* September 1993, pp. 290–91, 315–18.
6. Suzanne Abraham and Derek Llewellyn-Jones, *Eating Disorders: The Facts.* New York: Oxford University Press, 4th ed., 1997, pp. 107–108.
7. Michael Maloney and Rachel Kranz, *Straight Talk About Eating Disorders.* New York: Facts On File, 1991, p. 3.
8. Maloney and Kranz, *Straight Talk About Eating Disorders,* p. 3.
9. Quoted in Jane E. Brody, "Personal Health: Help for Youths Beset by Eating Disorders," *New York Times,* January 31, 1996, p. C10.
10. Cherry Boone O'Neill, *Starving for Attention.* New York: Continuum, 1982, p. 37.
11. Quoted in Brody, "Personal Health: Help for Youths Beset by Eating Disorders," p. C10.
12. Joelle Attinger, Correspondent, CNN/IMPACT, March 15, 1998.
13. Quoted on CNN/IMPACT, March 15, 1998.

14. Marya Hornbacher, *Wasted: A Memoir of Anorexia and Bulimia.* New York: HarperFlamingo, 1998, p. 107.

15. Dixie Farley, "On the Teen Scene: Eating Disorders Require Medical Attention," *FDA Consumer,* March 1992, p. 27+. (www.ebscohost.com)

16. Leslie Morgan, "College—Food Fight: Eating Disorders on Campus," *Seventeen,* May 1993, p. 156.

17. Quoted in Eric Goodman, "The Pressure to Be Perfect," *Glamour,* January 1996, p. 155.

18. Quoted in Goodman, "The Pressure to Be Perfect," p. 179.

19. Goodman, "The Pressure to Be Perfect," p. 180.

20. Quoted in Michelle Marble, "Binge Eating Needs to Be Recognized as a Psychiatric Illness," *Women's Health Weekly,* November 18, 1996, p. 7. (www.ebscohost.com)

21. Mary Pipher, *Reviving Ophelia: Saving the Selves of Adolescent Girls.* New York: Ballantine Books, 1994, p. 12.

22. Pipher, *Reviving Ophelia,* p. 179.

Chapter 2: The Pressure to Be Thin

23. Quoted in "Food Forays in Battle of the Sexes," *USA Today Magazine,* March 1997, p. 8+. (www.ebscohost.com)

24. Pipher, *Reviving Ophelia,* p. 183.

25. Quoted in Nadya Labi, "Girl Power," *Time,* June 29, 1998, p. 62.

26. Quoted in Judy Mann, *The Difference—Discovering the Hidden Ways We Silence Girls: Finding Alternatives That Can Give Them a Voice.* New York: Warner Books, 1996, p. 186.

27. Jacquelyn Mitchard, "A Gorgeous Woman, Including Curves," *Orlando Sentinel,* May 21, 1998, p. E-6.

28. Judith Rodin, "The New Meaning of Thin," *Glamour,* May 1992, p. 224.

29. Susie Orbach, "Introduction to the New Edition," *Fat Is a Feminist Issue.* New York: Galahad Books, 1978; new introduction, New York: Berkley Publishing Group, 1994.

30. Jane R. Hirschmann and Carol H. Munter, *Overcoming Overeating.* New York: Ballantine Books, 1988, p. 41.

31. Naomi Wolf, *The Beauty Myth: How Images of Beauty Are Used Against Women.* New York: William Morrow, 1991, p. 187.

32. Quoted in Wolf, *The Beauty Myth,* p. 188.

33. Christine Alt, "Viewpoint," *Glamour,* March 1992, p. 150.

34. Quoted in Jane E. Brody, "Personal Health: Using the Mind's Eye to Combat Eating Disorders," *New York Times,* February 7, 1996, p. C9.

35. Quoted in Leslie Knowlton, "Eating Disorders in Males," *Mental Health Infosource (MHi),* September 1995. (www.mhsource.com/edu/psytimes/p950942.html)

36. Joan Ryan, *Little Girls in Pretty Boxes: The Making and Breaking of Elite Gymnasts and Figure Skaters.* New York: Doubleday, 1995, p. 65.

37. Joan Ryan, *Little Girls in Pretty Boxes,* pp. 6–7.

38. Merrell Noden, "Dying While Dieting to Win," *Sports Parents,* May 2, 1998, taken from *Sports Illustrated for Kids,* May 1998 supplement, p. 5. (www.ebscohost.com)

39. Quoted in Karen Duffy and Barbara Sgroi, "The Model Maker," *Cosmopolitan,* June 1998, p. 180.

40. Hornbacher, *Wasted,* pp. 51–52.

41. William Davis, "Let's Have No More Victims of the Thinness Disease," reprinted by Eating Disorders Awareness and Prevention (EDAP) from the *Philadelphia Inquirer,* Commentary, August 6, 1994.

Chapter 3: Other Causes of Eating Disorders

42. Quoted in O'Neill, *Starving for Attention,* p. 168.

43. Hornbacher, *Wasted,* p. 6.

44. Quoted in Michelle Marble, "Eating Disorders: Victims Often Mistake Out-of-Control for Control," *Women's Health Weekly,* December 4, 1995, p. 9+. (www.ebscohost.com)

45. Quoted in Marble, "Eating Disorders: Victims Often Mistake Out-of-Control for Control," p. 9+.

46. Jane E. Brody, "Risky Behaviors Develop Because of Low Self-Esteem," *News-Journal,* Daytona Beach, FL, December 13, 1997, p. 1D.

47. Quoted in Brody, "Risky Behaviors Develop Because of Low Self-Esteem," pp. 1D–2D.

48. Quoted on CNN/IMPACT, March 15, 1998.

49. Joanne Witkowski, M.D., telephone interview by author, April 16, 1998.

50. Quoted in Jean Callahan, "Cosmo's Update on Eating Disorders," *Cosmopolitan,* May 1996, p. 230+. (www.ebscohost.com)

51. Colleen Thompson, "Abuse and Eating Disorders," *Mirror-Mirror: Eating Disorders Shared Awareness,* revised April 8, 1998. (www.mirror-mirror.org/physex.htm)

52. Quoted in Callahan, "Cosmo's Update on Eating Disorders," p. 230+.

53. Brett Silverstein and Deborah Perlick, *The Cost of Competence: Why Inequality Causes Depression, Eating Disorders, and Illness in Women.* New York: Oxford University Press, 1995, p. 137.

54. Mackenzie Stroh, as told to John Searles, "I Was Just Pounds Away from Death," *Cosmopolitan,* October 1997, p. 219.

55. Peggy Claude-Pierre, *The Secret Language of Eating Disorders.* New York: Times Books, Random House, 1997, p. 25.

56. O'Neill, *Starving for Attention,* p. 26.

Chapter 4: Eating Disorders in Males

57. Colleen Thompson, "Men and Eating Disorders," *Mirror-Mirror: Eating Disorders Shared Awareness,* revised July 30, 1998. (www.mirror-mirror.org/men.htm)

58. Quoted in Knowlton, "Eating Disorders in Males."

59. "The Male Body: Is Rambo Our Best Choice?" *Highlights* (a publication of the Columbia University Health Service), Spring 1995. (www.alice.columbia.edu/hw32.html)

60. Pamela S. McKay Parks and Marsha H. Read, "Adolescent Male Athletes: Body Image, Diet, and Exercise," *Adolescence,* Fall 1997, pp. 593+. (www.ebscohost.com)

61. Susan S. Lang, "Male Athletes Also Engage in Dysfunctional Eating, a Study Team Finds," *Science News,* April

1994. (gopher://gopher.cornell.edu/00/.files/PRST_FILES/PRST049406)

62. Quoted in Jean Seligmann, "The Pressure to Lose," *Newsweek,* May 2, 1994, p. 60+. (www.ebscohost.com)

63. Daniel Slosberg, "My Story," *Males and Eating Disorders.* (www.primenet.com/~danslos/males/story.html)

64. Ann Kearney-Cooke and Paule Steichen-Asch, "Men, Body Image, and Eating Disorders." Quoted in Arnold E. Andersen, ed., *Males with Eating Disorders.* New York: Brunner/Mazol, 1990, pp. 58, 63.

65. Claudia Hammond, "Men Also Suffer from Eating Disorders," *Nando Times,* Nando.net, Scripps Howard, 1997. (www.techserver.com/newsroom/ntn/health/091997/health 20_24443_noframes.html) (Article no longer available on website.)

66. Thompson, "Men and Eating Disorders."

67. Quoted in Knowlton, "Eating Disorders in Males."

68. Quoted in "Eating Disorders Strike Men, Too," *Psychotherapy Letter,* April 1996, p. 1+. (www.ebscohost.com)

69. Quoted in "Eating Disorders Strike Men, Too."

Chapter 5: Dangers of Eating Disorders

70. Colleen Thompson, "Dangerous Methods of Weight Control," *Mirror-Mirror: Eating Disorders Shared Awareness,* revised July 30, 1998. (www.mirror-mirror.org/dangerou.htm)

71. LeAdelle Phelps and Ellen Bajorek, "Eating Disorders of the Adolescent: Current Issues in Etiology, Assessment, and Treatment," *School Psychology Review,* March 1991, p. 9+. (www.ebscohost.com)

72. O'Neill, *Starving for Attention,* p. 67.

Chapter 6: Treatment of Eating Disorders

73. O'Neill, *Starving for Attention,* pp. 49–50.

74. Debbie Allen, "A Battle Between Body and Mind," *Miami Valley Family Life,* Cox Custom Publishing, February 1998, p. 9.

75. Abraham and Llewellyn-Jones, *Eating Disorders: The Facts,* p. 75.

76. Witkowski, telephone interview by author, April 16, 1998.

77. Claude-Pierre, *The Secret Language of Eating Disorders,* p. 115.

78. Abraham and Llewellyn-Jones, *Eating Disorders: The Facts,* p. 74.

79. Quoted on CNN/IMPACT, March 15, 1998.

80. Abraham and Llewellyn-Jones, *Eating Disorders: The Facts,* p. 122.

81. Abraham and Llewellyn-Jones, *Eating Disorders: The Facts,* pp. 78–79.

Chapter 7: Prevention of Eating Disorders

82. Quoted in Tori DeAngelis, "Body-Image Problems Affect All Groups," *APA [American Psychological Association] Monitor,* March 1997. (www.apa.org/monitor/mar97/gender. html)

83. Eating Disorders Awareness and Prevention (EDAP), *Am I on My Way to an Eating Disorder?* (brochure), 1997.

84. Quoted in Sandra Frederick, "Image Really Is Everything," *News-Journal,* Daytona Beach, FL, December 13, 1997, p. 2D.

85. EDAP, "Eating Disorders Awareness Week," 1998. (http://members.aol.com/edapinc/edaw.html)

86. EDAP, "About EDAP's Media Advocacy Campaign," 1998. (http://members.aol.com/edapwatch/aboutmedia.html)

87. EDAP, "It's Time to Rant and Rave," 1998. (http://members.aol.com/edapwatch/rantrave.html)

88. EDAP, "It's Time to Rant and Rave."

89. EDAP, "It's Time to Rant and Rave."

90. EDAP, "It's Time to Rant and Rave."

91. EDAP, "It's Time to Rant and Rave."

92. Quoted in Walter Scott, "Walter Scott's Personality Parade," *Parade,* April 12, 1998, p. 2.

93. Quoted in Leslie Doolittle, "Names and Faces: Kate's Weighty Issues" (as quoted in *Jump* magazine), *Orlando Sentinel,* April 10, 1998, p. 2A.

94. Quoted in Dan Rather, "All Figured Out," *48 Hours,* February 26, 1998.

95. Quoted in Rather, "All Figured Out."

96. Quoted in Rather, "All Figured Out."

97. Quoted in Lisa Bannon, "Top-Heavy Barbie Is Getting Body Work at Hands of Mattel," *Wall Street Journal* (eastern edition), November 17, 1997, p. A10.

98. Karen Bokram, "Who's Making You Fat?" *Girls' Life,* June/July 1998, p. 53.

99. Michael Levine and Linda Smolak, "Tips for Kids on Eating Well and Feeling Good About Yourself," EDAP information sheet.

100. Jean Rubel, "Are You Finding What You Need?" in Lindsey Hall, *Full Lives: Women Who Have Freed Themselves from Food and Weight Obsession.* Carlsbad, CA: Gürze Books, 1993, p. 49.

Glossary

---

anorexia: An eating disorder in which a person has an irrational fear of getting fat and therefore diets excessively to stay thin. Such a person is referred to variously as an anoretic, anorectic, or anorexic.

behavioral therapy: Therapy that tries to change a person's behavior by giving rewards or privileges for appropriate behavior. For example, an anoretic who gains weight will be rewarded with something she likes.

binge: To eat or drink excessively.

binge eating: An eating disorder in which a person eats large quantities of food. A person who is binge eating feels out of control and cannot stop the behavior, even when he or she wants to quit.

Body Mass Index (BMI): A measurement designed to show whether a person is underweight, normal weight, or overweight. It is based on a relationship between height and weight. Although designed for the metric system (kilograms and meters), there is a formula for pounds and inches:

$$\frac{\text{weight in pounds} \times 703}{\text{height in inches} \times \text{height in inches}} = \text{Body Mass Index (BMI)}$$

bulimia: An eating disorder in which a person binges repeatedly and then works to offset the effects through vomiting, vigorous exercise, or the use of diuretics, laxatives, or strict dieting.

cognitive behavioral therapy: Therapy that tries to help a person change distorted ways of thinking.

compulsive behavior: Behavior in which a person cannot resist the impulse to act.

compulsive eating: Another term for binge eating. A person eats large quantities of food and feels out of control while doing so.

depression: Feelings of extreme sadness and hopelessness.

diuretic: A drug that makes the body lose water through urination.

laxative: A food or drug that stimulates the bowels.

neurochemical: Referring to the chemical composition and processes of the nervous system.

obsessive: Excessive or compulsive preoccupation with an idea or an unwanted feeling or emotion.

purge: To get rid of the contents of the stomach or bowels. In eating disorders, purging refers to getting rid of food or calories that can add weight to the body.

self-esteem: Feeling pride in oneself.

trauma: An emotional shock or wound that can damage a person psychologically.

Organizations
to Contact

American Anorexia Bulimia Association, Inc. (AABA)
165 West 46th St., Suite 1108
New York, NY 10036
(212) 575-6200
fax: (212) 278-0698
website: http://members.aol.com/AmAnBu
e-mail: amanbu@aol.com

The AABA is a national, nonprofit organization dedicated to the prevention and treatment of eating disorders. It provides a nationwide referral service of support groups and treatment centers. It also provides public information, school outreach, prevention programs, a college task force, research support, media support, and professional training.

Eating Disorders Awareness and Prevention, Inc. (EDAP)
603 Stewart St., Suite 803
Seattle, WA 98101
(206) 382-3587
fax: (206) 292-9890
websites: http://members.aol.com/edapinc
           http://members.aol.com/edapwatch/aboutmedia.html

EDAP is a national, nonprofit organization, founded in 1987, that promotes the awareness and prevention of eating disorders by encouraging positive self-esteem and acceptance of one's size. It maintains a central database of the latest information about eating disorders and provides educational information to schools, parents, and health professionals.

Gürze Books

P.O. Box 2238
Carlsbad, CA 92018
(800) 756-7533
fax: (760) 434-5476
website: www.gurze.com
e-mail: gzcatl@aol.com

Gürze Books provides information on eating disorders, including recovery, research, education, advocacy, and prevention. Its free *Eating Disorders Resource Catalogue* contains books with facts about eating disorders, self-help books, professional texts, and information about national organizations and treatment centers.

National Association of Anorexia Nervosa and Associated Disorders (ANAD)

Box 7
Highland Park, IL 60035
(847) 831-3438
fax: (847) 433-4632
website: http://members.aol.com/anad20/index.html
e-mail: anad20@aol.com

The first national, nonprofit, educational and self-help organization dedicated to helping those with eating disorders, ANAD offers many services, including free hot-line counseling, information and referrals, self-help and support groups for victims and parents, educational programs, and a listing of therapists, hospitals, and clinics treating eating disorders. ANAD also publishes a national newsletter, supports research, provides conferences on eating disorders, monitors advertisements and the media, and fights insurance discrimination. All of its services are free.

National Eating Disorders Organization (NEDO)

6655 South Yale Ave.
Tulsa, OK 74136
(918) 481-4044
fax: (918) 481-4076

websites: www.laureate.com
www.anred.com
e-mail: lpchnedo@ionet.net

NEDO was founded as the National Anorexic Aid Society (NAAS) in 1977 and later changed its name to the National Eating Disorders Organization (NEDO). In 1997, it was joined by Anorexia Nervosa and Related Eating Disorders (ANRED). Its purpose is to increase the understanding of all forms of eating disorders and obesity and to help prevent them. It offers educational and referral information and also has an international referral directory of over 900 treatment providers. Other services include an information packet, a national newsletter, information on starting a support group, and a five-day lesson plan for teaching about eating disorders.

Overeaters Anonymous (OA)
6075 Zenith Court, NE
Rio Rancho, NM 87124-6424
(505) 891-2664
fax: (505) 891-4320
website: www.OvereatersAnonymous.org
e-mail: overeatr@technet.nm.org

Overeaters Anonymous is a self-help organization based on the twelve-step program of Alcoholics Anonymous. It is not a diet club and does not weigh people or tell them what to eat. The only requirement for membership is a desire to stop eating compulsively. OA offers support in dealing with the physical and emotional symptoms of compulsive eating, and members support each other in taking "one day at a time."

Suggestions for Further Reading

Miriam Adderholdt-Elliot, *Perfectionism: What's Bad About Being Too Good?* Minneapolis, MN: Free Spirit, 1987. Discusses the difference between doing your best and overdoing it.

Kaz Cooke, *Real Gorgeous: The Truth About Body and Beauty.* New York: W. W. Norton, 1996. Gives practical ways to find real self-esteem. Uses jokes, cartoons, and humor to discuss eating disorders, body image, diet myths, and the media.

Michael Maloney and Rachel Kranz, *Straight Talk About Eating Disorders.* New York: Facts On File, 1991. Gives facts on eating disorders, including the biology of weight and the mixed messages girls get about food and looks.

Barbara Moe, *Coping with Eating Disorders.* Rev. ed. New York: The Rosen Publishing Group, 1995. Gives facts on eating disorders, including the role of families, the media, and society.

Cherry Boone O'Neill, *Dear Cherry: Questions and Answers on Eating Disorders.* New York: Continuum, 1985. O'Neill answers questions about eating disorders.

———, *Starving for Attention.* New York: Continuum, 1982. O'Neill tells the story of her own struggle with anorexia and bulimia and her eventual recovery.

Joan Ryan, *Little Girls in Pretty Boxes: The Making and Breaking of Elite Gymnasts and Figure Skaters.* New York: Doubleday, 1995. Discusses how these sports contribute to eating disorders and other problems in their participants.

Additional
Works Consulted

Books

Suzanne Abraham and Derek Llewellyn-Jones, *Eating Disorders: The Facts.* New York: Oxford University Press, 4th ed., 1997. Gives straightforward, scientific facts about adolescent eating behavior, the three major eating disorders (anorexia nervosa, bulimia, and compulsive eating), and obesity.

Arnold E. Andersen, ed., *Males with Eating Disorders.* New York: Brunner/Mazol, 1990. Contains articles on eating disorders in boys and men by a selection of researchers. One psychologist tells of his own struggle with bulimia.

Peggy Claude-Pierre, *The Secret Language of Eating Disorders.* New York: Times Books, Random House, 1997. The author discusses the struggles her two daughters had with eating disorders and explains the theories she developed about cause and treatment. She now uses those theories at her own clinic in Canada.

Robert J. Condon, *Great Women Athletes of the 20th Century.* Jefferson, NC: McFarland, 1991. Gives brief biographies of twentieth-century athletes.

Lindsey Hall, *Full Lives: Women Who have Freed Themselves from Food and Weight Obsession.* Carlsbad, CA: Gürze Books, 1993. Presents a collection of essays by women who have overcome problems with eating.

Jane R. Hirschmann and Carol H. Munter, *Overcoming Overeating.* New York: Ballantine Books, 1988. Examines cultural pressures that cause overeating and offers a plan for moving beyond a negative preoccupation with eating and body weight.

Marya Hornbacher, *Wasted: A Memoir of Anorexia and Bulimia.* New York: HarperFlamingo, 1998. Hornbacher presents a frank and detailed story of her troubled adolescence and long struggle with eating disorders.

Judy Mann, *The Difference—Discovering the Hidden Ways We Silence Girls: Finding Alternatives That Can Give Them a Voice.* New York: Warner Books, 1996. Discusses the negative messages our culture gives to girls, leading to feelings of low self-esteem, and offers ways to combat those messages.

Susie Orbach, *Fat Is a Feminist Issue.* New York: Galahad Books, 1978; new introduction, New York: Berkley Publishing Group, 1994. Discusses society's focus on women's body image and examines the emotional meanings of "fat," "thin," and "overweight."

Mary Pipher, *Reviving Ophelia: Saving the Selves of Adolescent Girls.* New York: Ballantine Books, 1994. Discusses the special problems teenage girls face growing up in America today.

Brett Silverstein and Deborah Perlick, *The Cost of Competence: Why Inequality Causes Depression, Eating Disorders, and Illness in Women.* New York: Oxford University Press, 1995. Using historic examples and recent studies, presents the authors' theory that inequality causes depression, eating disorders, and other illnesses in women.

Rhoda Unger and Mary Crawford, *Women and Gender: A Feminist Psychology.* New York: McGraw Hill, 1992. A psychology textbook that discusses women, gender, and the ways that race, ethnicity, class, sexual orientation, and age modify women's experiences.

Naomi Wolf, *The Beauty Myth: How Images of Beauty Are Used Against Women.* New York: William Morrow, 1991.

Discusses how women are urged to spend time, effort, and money trying to meet unrealistic standards of beauty.

Magazines, Newspapers, TV Documentaries, Brochures

Debbie Allen, "A Battle Between Body and Mind," *Miami Valley Family Life,* Cox Custom Publishing, February 1998.

Christine Alt, "Viewpoint," *Glamour,* March 1992.

American Anorexia Bulimia Association (AABA), information sheets.

Judith Anderson, "Battling Bulimia: My War Story," *Glamour,* September 1993.

Sandra Arbetter, MSW, "The A's and B's of Eating Disorders," *Current Health 2,* September 1994.

Candi D. Ashley, Joe F. Smith, James B. Robinson, and Mark T. Richardson, "Disordered Eating in Female Collegiate Athletes and Collegiate Females in an Advanced Program of Study: A Preliminary Investigation," *International Journal of Sport Nutrition,* December 6, 1996.

Lisa Bannon, "Top-Heavy Barbie Is Getting Body Work at Hands of Mattel," *Wall Street Journal* (eastern edition), November 17, 1997.

Karen Bokram, "Who's Making You Fat?" *Girls' Life,* June/July 1998.

Jane E. Brody, "Personal Health: Help for Youths Beset by Eating Disorders," *New York Times,* January 31, 1996.

———, "Personal Health: Using the Mind's Eye to Combat Eating Disorders," *New York Times,* February 7, 1996.

———, "Risky Behaviors Develop Because of Low Self-Esteem," *News-Journal,* Daytona Beach, FL, December 13, 1997.

Jean Callahan, "Cosmo's Update on Eating Disorders," *Cosmopolitan,* May 1996.

Gregory Cerio and Joyce Wagner, "A Glorious Day," *People,* October 24, 1994.

Veronica Chambers, "Fashion: Big Beautiful—And Hip," *Newsweek,* August 24, 1998.

CNN/IMPACT, March 15, 1998.

H. J. Cummins, "Weight Problems Ruining Teen Lives," *Plain Dealer,* Cleveland, OH, March 25, 1998.

John Darnton, "'Skeletal' Models Create Furor over British Vogue," *New York Times,* June 3, 1996.

William Davis, "Let's Have No More Victims of the Thinness Disease," reprinted by Eating Disorders Awareness and Prevention (EDAP) from the *Philadelphia Inquirer,* Commentary, August 6, 1994.

Leslie Doolittle, "Names and Faces: Kate's Weighty Issues," *Orlando Sentinel,* April 10, 1998.

Karen Duffy and Barbara Sgroi, "The Model Maker," *Cosmopolitan,* June 1998.

Eating Disorders Awareness and Prevention (EDAP), *Am I on My Way to an Eating Disorder?* (brochure), 1997.

"Eating Disorders Strike Men, Too," *Psychotherapy Letter,* April 1996.

"Eating Disorders Strike Younger Teens," *News-Journal,* Daytona Beach, FL, January 3, 1998.

Dixie Farley, "On the Teen Scene: Eating Disorders Require Medical Attention," *FDA Consumer,* March 1992.

"Food Forays in Battle of the Sexes," *USA Today Magazine,* March 1997.

Sandra Frederick, "Image Really Is Everything," *News-Journal,* Daytona Beach, FL, December 13, 1997.

Susan Gilbert, "More Men May Seek Eating-Disorder Help," *New York Times,* August 28, 1996.

Eric Goodman, "The Pressure to Be Perfect," *Glamour,* January 1996.

Todd Heatherton, Fary Mahamedi, Meg Striepe, Alison Field, and Pamela Keel, "A 10-Year Longitudinal Study of Body Weight, Dieting, and Eating Disorder Symptoms," *Journal of Abnormal Psychology,* vol. 106, no. 1, 1997.

Valli Herman, "Delta Burke Spins Scorn into Gold with New Book," *Orlando Sentinel,* April 23, 1998.

Susan Karlin, "Tracey Gold's Bright Future," *Redbook,* September 1997.

Mary Alice Kellogg, "Above the Curve," *In Style,* June 1997.

Debra Kent, "Sex + Body: Eating Disorders & Sex," *Seventeen,* October 1993.

Nadya Labi, "Girl Power," *Time,* June 29, 1998.

Michael Levine, "Summary of Findings Concerning Weight and Shape Concerns in Late Childhood and Adolescence." Information sheet from Eating Disorders Awareness and Prevention (EDAP) presented at the 13th national NEDO Conference, Columbus, OH, October 3, 1994. Also other informational sheets, such as "Tips for Kids on Eating Well and Feeling Good About Yourself" (written with Linda Smolak).

Michelle Marble, "Eating Disorders: Binge Eating Needs to Be Recognized as a Psychiatric Illness," *Women's Health Weekly,* November 18, 1996.

———, "Eating Disorders: Victims Often Mistake Out-of-Control for Control," *Women's Health Weekly,* December 4, 1995.

Kelli McNeill, "Starving for Attention," *American Fitness,* July/August 1995.

Jacquelyn Mitchard, "A Gorgeous Woman, Including Curves," *Orlando Sentinel,* May 21, 1998.

Leslie Morgan, "College—Food Fight: Eating Disorders on Campus," *Seventeen,* May 1993.

National Association of Anorexia Nervosa and Associated Disorders (ANAD), information sheets.

Merrell Noden, "Dying While Dieting to Win," *Sports Parents,* May 2, 1998, taken from *Sports Illustrated for Kids,* May 1998 supplement.

Eric Pace, "Obituary: Christy Henrich, 22, Gymnast Who Suffered from Anorexia," *New York Times,* July 28, 1994.

Pamela S. McKay Parks and Marsha H. Read, "Adolescent Male Athletes: Body Image, Diet, and Exercise," *Adolescence,* Fall 1997.

LeAdelle Phelps and Ellen Bajorek, "Eating Disorders of the Adolescent: Current Issues in Etiology, Assessment, and Treatment," *School Psychology Review,* March 1991.

Dan Rather, *48 Hours,* CBS News, February 26, 1998.

Judith Rodin, "The New Meaning of Thin," *Glamour,* May 1992.

Walter Scott, "Walter Scott's Personality Parade," *Parade,* April 12, 1998.

Lisa Schwarzbaum, "Fergie's Follies," *McCall's,* June 1997.

Jean Seligmann, "The Pressure to Lose," *Newsweek,* May 2, 1994.

Mackenzie Stroh, as told to John Searles, "I Was Just Pounds Away from Death," *Cosmopolitan,* October 1997.

"Treating Eating Disorders," *Harvard Women's Health Watch,* May 1996.

Kathryn J. Zerbe, "Eating Disorders in the 1990s: Clinical Challenges and Treatment Implications," *Bulletin of the Menninger Clinic,* vol. 56, no. 2, 1992.

Websites

Tori DeAngelis, "Body-Image Problems Affect All Groups," *APA [American Psychological Association] Monitor,* March 1997. (www.apa.org/monitor/mar97/gender.html)

Eating Disorders Awareness and Prevention (EDAP), "About EDAP's Media Advocacy Campaign," EDAP, 1998. (http://members.aol.com/edapwatch/aboutmedia.html)

———, "Eating Disorders Awareness Week," EDAP, 1998. (http://members.aol.com/edapinc/edaw.html)

———, "It's Time to Rant and Rave," EDAP, 1998. (http://members.aol.com/edapwatch/rantrave.html)

Claudia Hammond, "Men Also Suffer From Eating Disorders," *Nando Times,* Nando.net, Scripps Howard, 1997. (www.techserver.com/newsroom/ntn/health/091997/health20_24443_noframes.html)

Leslie Knowlton, "Eating Disorders in Males," *Mental Health Infosource (MHi),* September 1995. (www.mhsource.com/edu/psytimes/ p950942.html)

Susan S. Lang, "Male Athletes Also Engage in Dysfunctional Eating, a Study Team Finds," *Science News,* April 1994. (gopher://gopher.cornell.edu/00/.files/PRST_FILES/PRST049406)

"The Male Body: Is Rambo Our Best Choice?" *Highlights* (a publication of the Columbia University Health Service), Spring 1995. (www.alice.columbia.edu/hw32.html)

Daniel Slosberg, "My Story," *Males and Eating Disorders.* (www.primenet.com/~danslos/males/story.html)

Colleen Thompson, *Mirror-Mirror: Eating Disorders Shared Awareness. (*www.mirror-mirror.org/eatdis.htm)

Index

Picture Credits

About the Author

Elizabeth Weiss Vollstadt has extensive experience writing about medical issues. In addition to freelance work, she spent several years as Manager of Publications for Rainbow Babies and Childrens Hospital in Cleveland, Ohio, where she wrote and produced brochures, newsletters, a consumer magazine, and a one-hundred-year history of the hospital. She holds a B.A. from Adelphi University and an M.A. from John Carroll University, both in English. Her stories for young people have appeared in publications such as the *Highlights for Children* anthologies, *Children's Digest, Jack and Jill, My Friend,* and *The Christian Family Christmas Book.* She has also taught English and writing to students from grade seven through college. She now lives in DeLand, Florida, with her husband, where she divides her time between writing and boating on the Saint Johns River.